NIGHT FLYING IN SINGLE-ENGINE AIRPLANES

Other TAB Books by the author:

NIGHT FLYING IN SINGLE-ENGINE AIRPLANES

BY PAUL GARRISON

MODERN AVIATION SERIES

TAB BOOKS

BLUE RIDGE SUMMIT, PA. 17214

FIRST EDITION

FIRST PRINTING—JULY 1979

Copyright © 1979 by TAB BOOKS

Printed in the United States of America

Library of Congress Cataloging in Publication Data

Garrison, Paul.
    Night flying in single-engine airplanes.

    Includes index.
    1. Night flying. I. Title.
TL711.N5G37   629.132'52'43   79-14385
ISBN 0-8306-9789-6
ISBN 0-8306-2266-7 pbk.

Cover photo courtesy of Don Downie.

Contents

Preface

Into the Blackness Which Is Night

It is a quarter past nine. The business meeting had lasted longer than he had anticipated, and then he'd let them talk him into joining them for dinner. He would have liked to have joined them in a drink too, but had decided against it, knowing that it was important for him to fly home tonight.

The pilot, let's for the sake of argument call him Frank Townsend, is 48 years old, married with two teenage children, and has been flying for close to two years, accumulating some 150 hours in the left seat. He is the sole owner of a small but successful business and it was his need to travel frequently which caused him to take flying lessons and subsequently to buy the Piper Arrow which is now waiting in its tiedown spot at the small private airport just east of town.

Frank is a conservative, careful pilot who prides himself on not taking any unnecessary chances, and all of his 150 hours, except for less than one, were flown during daylight hours in VFR conditions. His one and only experience with night flying consists of about 45 or 50 minutes when, accompanied by his instructor, he flew a series of touch-and-go landings at his home airport after sunset but before complete darkness had set in.

Like every pilot, Frank knows, of course, or at least he has been told, that it is virtually impossible to land an airplane at night except on a lighted airport, and that, in the unlikely event of an engine failure, he would more probably than not be in very serious trouble. It is for this reason that he has, to date, avoided flying at night, but today it just can't be helped. Getting home before tomorrow is too important.

On his way in the rented car to the Bermuda Dunes Airport he mentally goes over the route he will be flying back to Bakersfield. A straight line and, obviously, the shortest route from Bermuda Dunes (near Indio, California) to Bakersfield goes right smack over the tops of the San Gorgonio mountains, over 10,000 feet high, and representing what might be described as unfriendly terrain, even in daylight. If he detoured to the right and then passed the higher mountains to the north, he'd be over more or less level desert until reaching the southern portion of the Sierra Nevada. If, on the other hand, he detoured left, he'd be flying over much of the Los Angeles Basin and would then be crossing the mountains north of L.A. near the Gorman VOR. Or he could compromise and fly through Cajon Pass. Well, once at the airport he'd check the weather and make up his mind.

The airport is deserted, the FBO having closed up shop for the night. He drives the car to the airplane and by the light of the headlights stashes his luggage. He then drives the car to a parking place and slips the keys and rental-agreement copy through the mail slot of the FBO office. Then, depositing the appropriate change in the pay phone, he dials the flight service station at Palm Springs.

"Flight Service, Muller."

"Yeah, say, this is Cherokee Arrow One Two Four Niner Whiskey. I'm at Bermuda Dunes. Could you give me the weather for the next couple of hours between here and Bakersfield, please."

"Stand by one." Pause. "Palm Springs, ten thousand overcast, visibility three zero. Which route are you planning to go? Via Palmdale or south around the mountains?"

"It depends. Could you give me the weather for both?"

"Okay, Los Angeles, sky partially obscured in smoke and haze, visibility one. Burbank measured ceiling two thousand, visibility two in haze. Palmdale twelve thousand overcast, visibility four zero, and, stand by for Bakersfield." Pause. "Current Bakersfield weather four thousand broken, ten thousand overcast, visibility eight, light drizzle. And they are forecasting no change until four a.m. when they're expecting fog with visibilities occasionally below one mile."

"Okay, thanks."

"Would you like to file a flight plan?"

"Well, yes, maybe I better." He goes ahead and files a VFR flight plan, estimating his time en route as one hour and 40 minutes. "How about the winds aloft?"

"Winds aloft at six and niner thousand, light and variable, at one, two thousand two seven zero degrees at one zero."

"Thanks. I'll call you when I'm off."

"Roger."

He walks back to the airplane to do the habitual preflight, wishing he had a flashlight. With only the fairly dim runway lights illuminating the area, he has to stick his finger into the tanks to make sure they are full. They are. In order to check the oil he finds that he has to take the dipstick to one of the runway lights to be able to see whether there is an adequate amount of oil. There is.

He removes the chocks and tiedown ropes, climbs in and closes the door. After fastening his seatbelt he starts the engine, taxis to the nearest end of the one runway since the windsock is hanging limply, indicating no wind to worry about. He does his runup and exercises the prop and controls, drops his flaps one notch, and pulls onto the runway. And now, for the first time in his flying career, he realizes what little illumination his landing light affords him. But with the runway lights on either side stretching ahead for the full 3,500 feet, he feels comfortable and advances the throttle, at the same time releasing the brakes. The little airplane accelerates, rotates, lifts off, climbs smoothly, propelling its pilot into another sensation, never before experienced—total darkness.

The effect is sudden and, when experienced for the first time, rather shocking. With the high overcast blocking whatever light might be available from moon or starts, there is nothing, absolutely nothing to look at, especially with the aircraft in climb and its nose in the way of any lights on the ground.

Frank becomes uncomfortably aware of the damp in the palms of his hands. He takes a deep breath and talks to himself. "Relax! One thing at a time! Reduce manifold pressure to twenty-three inches." He does. "Now the prop back to twenty-three hundred rmp. Okay, Flaps up. Oh, Christ, I still have the landing light on." He pushes the rocker switch to off, then tunes his com radio to 122.1 and his nav receiver to 115.5 and calls Palm Springs to open his flight plan.

Through the window on his left side the lights of Palm Springs come into view and way up ahead a band of slowly moving lights, the freeway, stretches west toward Los Angeles.

Frank can't remember having ever felt quite so alone and cut off from the world. Also, except for a few cursory exercises under the hood during flight training, he has never before been called upon to fly his airplane entirely by reference to the instruments. There is no friendly horizon to reassure him that his wings are level. Only the artificial horizon and turn-and-bank indicator prove that he is, indeed, flying straight ahead and the vertical-speed needle holds steady on 400 fpm up.

He has spread his Los Angeles Sectional across his lap and, unable to see by the red instrument lights, has turned on the dome light. The route he has decided to fly follows the freeway through Beaumont Pass to San Bernadino, then north, following another freeway through Cajon Pass and then northwest to Palmdale. From there follow the 299-degree radial of the Palmdale VOR over the top of a nearly 8,000-foot-high mountain range straight into Bakersfield. He is, of course, aware that there are mountains on either side of the first part of this route, reaching all the way up to over 10,000 feet, and he wishes desperately that he could see them but, except for the highway below, everything is coal black in all directions.

Oh, there are occasional specks of light here and there, but not enough to give an indication of the terrain.

The TO reading in the OBI has changed to FROM, indicating that he has left Palm Springs behind. He is now flying level at 6,500 feet, staying right above the busy freeway and heading just about straight west into the Beaumont Pass, uncomfortably aware that the blackness on either side hides jagged rocks rising steeply from the desert floor to elevations several thousand feet above his current level of flight. But as long as the freeway lights are clearly visible below and ahead, he assures himself that there cannot possibly be an obstacle in his way.

Some miles ahead the crisp brilliance of the individual headlights below changes to a soft milklike stream of white. The infamous Los Angeles smog starts to hide the details below, but enough illumination seeps through to indicate the direction of the road.

With the reading from the Palm Springs VOR becoming erratic, he turns some 30 degrees to the right to head straight for Norton Air Force Base.

While, according to his chart, the Cajon Pass never rises much above 3,000 feet, it is ringed closely, too close for comfort, by 5,000 and 6,000-foot peaks, and Frank decides to roll the trim back and to cruise-climb to 8,500 in order to be well clear of everything except, of course, the San Gabriel Mountains which should remain some distance to his left.

Suddenly what appears to be a simply immense array of pulsating strobe lights enters his field of vision from above left, streaks past, curves to the right in front of him descending rapidly in the direction of Norton. "Probably one of those C-141s they fly out of there," he explains to himself. "I hope, the hell, they at least look where they're going." He turns and looks as far back as he can see, but there is nothing else.

The lights of San Bernardino, diluted by smog, lie straight ahead like a milky pie with a spike sticking out beyond, carrying hopeful throngs of gamblers from Los Angeles to Las Vegas and elated winners and deflated losers the other way.

Frank heads for that spike, knowing it to be the highway on which he will depend to lead him through Cajon Pass and into Antelope Valley and the Mojave Desert. He is level now at 8,500 and the lights of what would seem to be another light aircraft pass below in the opposite direction.

All of a sudden and quite without warning the lights below, all lights in fact, disappear, being replaced by an intense red and green glow at his wingtips punctuated by blue-white flashes from his own strobe. It takes him a moment or two to realize that he has flown into a cloud. Noticeably shaken, he tries to decide what to do. Climb? Descend? Turn back? He certainly doesn't want to turn back, and he hates the idea of dropping down lower with all those rocks sticking up all over the place. That leaves climbing, but how does he know that he won't be climbing into even more clouds?

Before he has time to take any of those actions he is in the clear again. It was just a lonely little cloud sitting there all by itself. Or was it? How do you tell? He strains his eyes, looking straight ahead, trying to see a variation in the shades of dark-grey-black, but there is none. Well, let's just say it was a warning. It happened once and it can happen again.

The road below makes a sharp dogleg and then veers off to the right. At the same time his nav receiver starts to pick up the signal from the Palmdale VOR which, his OBI reading tells him, calls for a heading of 285 degrees. He adjusts his direction of flight and, keeping the needle centered, flies on. If it only wasn't so damn black. Right now he'd give a month's pay for a full moon. There is something creepy about the knowledge that you're racing at 150 miles per hour toward an unseen nothing.

After a while small breaks begin to appear in the high overcast ahead, and it makes him feel better to see some stars up there in the sky. He doesn't really know why it makes him feel better. It just does. Somehow those few specks of light way up there make the night less forbidding.

Keeping the OBI needle conscientiously centered he flies on toward Palmdale, more relaxed now that he feels certain that, for the time being, at least, there are no more mountains to worry about. As a matter of fact, he is technically high enough to cross the Sierra Nevada between Palmdale and Bakersfield, but only just, and he knows that once he gets closer to that area, he'll climb to a somewhat higher level, probably 10,500 or something like that.

With nothing to do other than holding the wings level and watching the needle, his mind begins to wander back to the events of the day, the business meeting which turned out better than he had expected. Once that would start to pay off, maybe he would be able to afford at least a simple autopilot. It sure would make flights like the one tonight a lot easier. But then, of course, there are Andrea's teeth to be considered, and his wife had been bugging him to get rid of that eight-year-old Chevrolet, though it is doing just fine and he is perfectly happy with it. Funny, in the days before he learned to fly, just about once every year or two he would get that bug to trade the car for a newer model. No more. Cars don't mean a thing any more other than a convenient means to get to the market or the airport. In those days it was his wife who used to argue that they couldn't afford a new car, and then he'd go and get one anyway. And now it is she who wants to get involved with another set of those endless car payments while he is perfectly delighted to drive that old clunker. At least it's free and clear.

Oh well, you never know. Maybe there'll be enough profit in that deal to take care of Andrea's teeth and Elaine's new car plus that autopilot. Oh, he knows he is probably being overly optimistic, but why not? It sure couldn't happen to a more deserving guy.

Damn, what happened to that needle. He suddenly realizes that it is pegged all the way to the right.

Without noticing it he'd drifted left of his course and left is where the mountains are. Nervously he stares out of the window to his left but there is nothing to look at. He corrects to the right and adjusts the OBS until the needle is centered again. Three hundred degrees! How did he manage to get that far off course?

He looks up to get a glimpse of those friendly stars, but there aren't any. Apparently the overcast is solid again. Well, as long as it stays up there, he wouldn't worry about it, not much, anyway.

As he gazes from side to side, trying to see something recognizable, he suddenly picks up the impression of a rotating beacon, green and white. He looks toward it, but can't see it any more.

"I could have sworn..."

But he can't find it again, not until he starts to look elsewhere. Then, there it is again, one green, two white, one green. Palmdale! And then he remembers someone having told him once that at night you've got a blind spot when looking straight ahead. He can't remember exactly why, but by slowly moving his eyes from side to side he is now able to keep the rotating beacon in sight.

As he gets closer it becomes easier to keep the rotating beacon in sight and after another ten minutes or so he can see not only the airport lights but the lights of the towns of Palmdale and Lancaster beyond.

He calls the Palmdale FSS and asks for the Palmdale and Bakersfield weather. Neither has changed appreciably during the last hour.

When he finally crosses the VOR he adjusts his OBS to 299 degrees which should, according to his chart get him straight into Bakersfield. He's only got a little under 80 miles to go, barely more than a half an hour. But there are the Tehachapi mountains with at least one peak right on his route sticking up to 7,780 feet and another right next to it at 7,981 feet.

Better start climbing. No point waiting until the last minute. He rolls back the trim and, losing some airspeed, starts up at about 250 fpm or so. At that rate he figures it will take him about eight minutes to get up to 10,500, but there is plenty of time.

The air is starting to get a bit bumpy and he decides that there must be a westerly wind blowing over the mountains which would explain the turbulence east of the range.

Good thing he did start to climb when he did. Closer in it might have gotten kind of ugly down lower.

He is now beginning to worry about that cloud situation in Bakersfield. Four thousand broken, 10,000 overcast, light drizzle. The elevation at Bakersfield is about 500 feet, that means that if the ceiling is actually at 10,000 agl, it will be 10,500 msl, or just the altitude at which he'll be crossing the mountains. At Palmdale they said that the overcast is at 12,000. Right now he is climbing through 9,800 and as best as he can tell there are no clouds anywhere near.

Well, let's keep our fingers crossed that if the ceiling lowers between here and there, that it'll do it after I get across those rocks. Which reminds me, if it stays this dark and I can't see them, I better figure out a way to know when I'm past those peaks. Oh, a DME sure would be nice, but that costs nearly twice as much as an autopilot. Forget it.

Well, maybe when I get closer I can pick up the Gorman VOR. If that works, then all I've got to do is tune in the 020-degree radial, and when the needle centers I know I'm out of the woods.

Finally level at 10,500 feet, he tries for Gorman, tuning the second nav receiver to 116.1 and finds himself surprised but pleased when it gives a positive reading.

Let's see where I am right now.

He twists the OBS and the needle centers when he hits the 062-degree radial.

Getting close. By mentally drawing a line on the chart he now figures he is only about 15 miles from the highest point on his route. In other words, in less than 10 minutes he can start letting down.

That's another thing. How am I going to see those broken clouds they keep saying are around 4,000 feet? Well, no point worrying about that now. I'll just somehow cross that bridge when I get to it.

He has changed the OBS setting for Gorman to 020 degrees and the needle is comfortably pegged on the right. On the other OBI, the one tuned to Palmdale, the needle remains centered on the 299-degree radial, though for some minutes now he has been aware of having to hold about a 10-degree correction to the right in order to stay on course. Apparently there is quite a bit of wind out of the north. No wonder, earlier when he wasn't paying any attention, he had drifted off to the south.

By looking down he thinks he can make out the mountains below, and there is a red light down there, but he can't tell how far below it is.

The needle on the OBI tuned to Gorman starts to tremble. Splitting his attention between the two OBIs and the artificial horizon he flies on, paying little attention to what, if anything, is going on outside.

Just as the needle finally moves off the peg and starts to wander slowly toward the center, he is suddenly aware of the intense red and green halo surrounding his wingtips. Clouds! Dammit to hell, why couldn't they have waited another minute or two?

So I'm in the clouds. So what's the difference, really I can't see anything anyway. Better in the clouds than in the rocks, that's for sure!

Stubbornly he flies on, watching his instruments to be sure to stay on course and to keep the wings level.

Finally the Gorman needle has centered. He knows that the terrain below is now falling off sharply, but just to play safe he waits another minute or so before throttling back to start the descent. It's another 30 or 35 miles to Bakersfield. The pattern altitude there is about 1,500 feet, so he's got to lose 9,000 feet in, say, 15 minutes. That figures out to some 600 fpm down, and with a bit of fiddling with throttle and trim he succeeds in getting the VSI to indicate a steady 600 fpm.

He has been so busy, he hasn't even noticed that the red and green glow around his wingtips has disappeared. He's in the clear again, but now the other OBI, the one tuned to Palmdale, shows an OFF lag, and he quickly tunes to 115.4, Bakersfield and finds it reading 302 degrees TO, partically right on course. He twists the Gorman OBS to 330 which would mean that when both needles are centered, he should be right over the Bakersfield airport.

Not that he expects to actually need to use those nav aids. There is a distinct light glow right over his nose. That has to be Bakersfield, and once he gets close he figures it should be fairly simple to find the airport, knowing that it is located at the extreme northeast edge of town.

He is now coming down through 7,000 feet and he tunes his com radio at 118.1, Bakersfield Tower which comes in loud and clear, giving takeoff clearance to a Bonanza.

"Bakersfield Tower, Cherokee One Two Four Niner Whiskey, two five southwest, descending through seven, landing Bakersfield."

"Cherokee Four Niner Whiskey, Bakersfield, wind three four zero degrees at eight, altimeter two niner eight three, Runway Three Zero Right, report three-mile final."

"Four Niner Whiskey."

What ever happened to those broken clouds? Right now he can see the lights of Bakersfield quite clearly and there doesn't seem to be a cloud in sight anywhere.

Wrong again. Quite suddenly the lights tun into soup and then disappear altogether, and now he can actually see some dark shape and before he can decide what to do about it he's in it. He glances at the altimeter. It reads 5,500. Shouldn't take more than a minute to get out of this thing, he reasons, and concentrates on his instruments. And, sure enough, by the time he passes through 4,700 he's back in the clear with Bakersfield a brilliant field of lights straight ahead, and now, being below the broken clouds, he can see the reflection of the lights on their bases. A greyish mess with many large dark areas, which are probably the clear areas between the clouds.

By the time he reaches the outskirts of the city he is down to 3,000. He throttles back and trims the nose up to bleed off some speed, drops the gear and a notch of flaps and then calls Bakersfield Tower to say that he estimates his position as three miles from the airport.

"Cleared to land."

Suddenly aware that this will be the first honest-to-goodness night landing he has ever made, he carefully double-checks everything, but everything seems to be just fine. He crosses the threshold, pulls the throttle to idle, hauls back on the yoke and feels the wheels touch ground.

Home!

Chapter 1
What's So Different About Night?

What's so different is that it's dark out. That's about all. The airplane doesn't know the difference, and neither do its instruments or the multitude of navigational aids available to the pilot. So why all this fuss about night flying? The basic and primary answer is that you can't land an airplane in the dark. In other words, if a pilot is forced to land where no lighted airport is available, he is in rather serious trouble.

Let's start out by admitting that all flying is a calculated risk. But then, so is getting up in the morning. The difference with flying is that it requires a greater degree of precision and proficiency than most other pursuits. In order to fly we use some relatively complicated technology in an attempt to negate one of the most basic laws of nature, that of gravity.

This technology has resulted in a machine which can climb into the air, cruise at most any altitude, and descend at will, as long as it maintains a certain speed. To maintain this speed it needs power in the form of an engine and a propeller (or a jet engine). If the engine should, for any reason, fail to operate, the only other means of maintaining speed is to glide which must, necessarily, eventually bring us back to the ground. In daylight that is no problem. Airplanes glide very well (with some exceptions). Even a moderately proficient pilot should be able to glide his airplane to a safe landing, as long as he can see where he is going.

In years past, when aircraft engines were known to malfunction with depressing regularity and emergency dead-stick landings were commonplace, it was this fear of being forced to glide down into a black unknown which caused pilots to restrict their flying to the daylight hours. But today's engines, assuming they are well maintained, adequately lubricated and fed the right sort of fuel, have developed an uncanny degree of reliability and engine failures due to purely mechanical reasons are a rarity. Usually when we hear of an engine failure, it is due to some mismanagement by the pilot: Forgetting to switch from an empty to a full fuel tank; failing to lean the mixture when taking off from a high-altitude airport on a hot day; failing to apply carburetor heat in time when the carburetor begins to ice up. All in all there are an amazing number of stupid things a pilot can do, or clever things he can fail to do, which can result in sudden and complete loss of power.

If flying, then, is a calculated risk, night flying, too, is a calculated risk and to a fractionally greater degree. And if flying in general is not very forgiving of sloppy performance by the pilot, night flying is considerably less so. And this is not just restricted to making sure than the prop keeps on turning. It has to do with preflight preparation, with navigation, fuel management, knowing how to use the capabilities of one's eyes to their fullest under limited light conditions, knowing how to take full advantage of the instruments in the airplane, knowing how to recognize, or better still, anticipate

Preflight preparation is especially important before starting off into the night.

18

What is so different about night is that it's dark out.

weather, and, in the final analysis, knowing how to land an airplane by reference to whatever limited lighting might be available at the destination airport.

A year has 8,760 hours and of these a little less than half (depending on where you live) are hours of darkness. An airplane is a big investment, and if it is to justify the expenditure, it can't be expected to remain unused during all those hours, expecially during the winter months when hours of daylight are all too few. So, in the following pages we will go into quite considerable detail about everything that is involved in making night flight safe. And this might be the place for me to point out that over a period of some 20 years I have flown over 1,500 hours at night, most of them in single-engine airplanes, and I credit the fact that I am sitting here and writing this to a combination of two facts: The reliability of the modern aircraft engine, and a personal awareness of the demands which night flight makes of the pilot.

Chapter 2
The Fear of Night Flying

Only an excessively macho type pilot would deny that for all of us a certain amount of fear is part of flying (and he would be lying). The old saw about flying consisting of hours of utter boredom punctuated by moments of sheer terror is not too far from the truth. Anyone who has never been afraid in an airplane can't have done much flying. Even 20,000-hour airline captains, when pressed, will admit that a degree of fear is an integral part of their profession.

Night tends to make everything worse. The boring part is more boring than it is in the daytime when there is at least something to look at. And boredom coupled with fatigue can be a bad combination. But it's not the boring part that is particularly troublesome, assuming we manage to keep awake. It is that moment of fear when we suddenly realize that something isn't the way it should be. And it is not the fear itself that gets us into trouble, it is the panic which is its result.

Panic affects reasoning power. Suddenly we seem to be completely incapable of logical thought, of thinking even the simplest problem through to its solution. The most uncomplicated tasks, such as trying to figure out the reciprocal of a heading, become monstrously difficult to solve. We make little mistakes, first one, then another, until eventually what started out as a minor error grows into a major issue. And once panic has set in, there is little a person can do about it.

The trick, of course, is to never let fear develop into panic. Easier said than done? Well, not really. The first step in the right direction is to always stay ahead of the airplane. What is meant by that is that we never, for even a moment, stop flying the airplane and instead letting it fly us. Total awareness of what's going on at all times and what the necessary next step will be protects us from getting into unsuspected situations. This includes knowing what we would do, if the prevailing situation suddenly changes.

ENGINE SUDDENLY QUITS

For instance, if the engine suddenly quits, don't simply go diving helter skelter toward that lighted runway that, luckily, happens to be right off your left. Switch tanks, turn on the fuel pump. Most probably it'll start right up again. The number of pilots who crash airplanes each year, thinking the engine had given up the ghost when, in fact, they simply ran out of fuel in one tank, is both amazing and depressing. The fact is that a well-maintained engine doesn't suddenly stop cold without giving some warning. And if in the recent past it's been running rough or given some trouble, then you have no business being up in the air with it, especially at night.

SUDDENLY LOSE POWER

For instance, if you're suddenly losing power without any changes in the setting of the power levers, the first reaction should not be one of nervous shock, but simply a pull on the carburetor-heat knob. Carburetor ice can form on a warm summer night (or day) and when it does, it usually does so with great rapidity. Don't ever use partial carburetor heat, pull it all the way out and leave it out. At the same time you might lean the mixture a bit more to adjust for the enriching effect of carburetor heat. If you haven't waited too long the ice will melt off (causing the engine to briefly run rough) and after a while close to full power will be restored. But remember, if you are flying in conditions which have caused the icing in the first place, you most probably continue to be in such conditions for a while, and you may have to continue to fly with carburetor heat and accept the slight reduction in power and speed which results. You're a lot better off going slow than suddenly not going at all.

OFF FLAG POPS UP

For instance, the OFF flag suddenly pops up on your OBI while you could have sworn that you were within easy reception distance of the VOR to which you are tuned. First check the circuit breaker (or fuse). It may have popped. If that doesn't do it, switch frequencies to another VOR. VORs have been know to suddenly develop trouble. It doesn't happen often, but the reason for the OFF flag could be the fact that the station has had a interruption in its transmitter.

BANKING IN ONE DIRECTION

For instance, you've been letting the autopilot fly the airplane while you've relaxed, listening to some Country and Western music on the ADF. Suddenly the right wing drops out from under you. Probably the reason is that the autopilot was coupled to a VOR and is flying right over it. In that case the airplane will right itself automatically without any help from you. If that isn't the reason, then something may have gone awry in the servo-motor circuit. In other words, if it continues to bank in one direction, shut the thing off and start hand-flying the airplane. (I remember an autopilot in a Comanche that used to do that from time to time. It would fly fine for hours, then suddenly go crazy. They never could get it fixed right, but it sure kept me on my toes.)

HOW CLOSE TO GROUND

For instance, you're flying under a reasonably low overcast, but the visibility is good and, so far at least, there seems to be ample

But meanwhile the undercast is getting higher and higher...

room between the clouds and the ground. But after a while you begin to realize that either the ground is getting higher or the ceiling is getting lower. From the very moment you started flying under the overcast, you should have mentally made a decision as to how close to the ground you are willing to fly. It's purely a matter of personal judgment, though flying at less than 1,000 feet agl at night is asking for trouble. Anyway, whatever you have decided, be it 1,000, 2,000, 5,000, whatever, stick to it. Don't change your mind when the time comes to decide whether to go on, land or turn back. Then, when the space between ceiling and ground gets a bit skimpy, you don't end up nervously crawling along, hoping against hope that it'll get better. If it drops below your personal minimums, turn back or land. (Do remember, though, if you ever do get yourself into a tight corner with the clouds having closed in around you and the ground too close for comfort without a place to land, don't go scooting around at treetop level at night, hoping that by some stroke of dumb luck you're going to stumble on an airport. The only sensible thing to do is climb. The hell with the clouds. It may not be legal, but being alive is a lot better than legal. And it goes without saying that you know how to fly by instruments, otherwise, what are you doing up there at night in the first place? Then, as soon as you get high enough to reach someone on your radio, call the nearest FSS or ARTCC and file IFR. Even if you're not actually instrument rated, you'll do yourself and everybody a big favor by letting ATC know where you are, so they can make sure that you don't run into anyone or vice versa.)

HOW HIGH TO CLIMB

For instance, the opposite situation begins to develop. You're above a solid undercast, knowing that your destination is VFR and forecast to remain so. But meanwhile the undercast keeps getting higher and higher and you don't have any oxygen on board. Again, decide beforehand how high you're willing to go. And while you're still climbing, trying to get over that next ridge of clouds ahead, watch your airspeed. It's difficult to judge the attitude of the aircraft at night with clouds obscuring anything that could pass for a horizon. Don't suddenly stall out and possibly drop down into that mess. It's a lot easier to do than you would think. In this case, make certain you remember where the clouds began. Remember, if you reach your altitude limit at a point too far into the trip to be able to turn back and get back to at least broken conditions with the remaining fuel on board, you may find yourself forced to go IFR (and file, please!)

It cannot be emphasized too strongly that knowing in advance what one will do if something untoward develops, reduces the chance that fear will turn to panic. Virtually any emergency can be handled and eventually overcome, if one remains calm and collected. That doesn't mean that there is anything wrong with being afraid. Only a fool knows no fear.

Chapter 3
A Calculated Risk

Life is full of calculated risks, risks we know we are taking when we do, but which we believe to be worth taking for one reason or another. When we drive our cars we know that chances are that someone will run into us and cause serious injury or worse. But driving is faster and more convenient than walking, so we drive. When we light a cigarette we know that it represents a risk to our well being, but we enjoy smoking and therefore accept the risk as worth it. Just about every sort of sport, skiing, boating, hunting, yes, even golf, involves a degree of risk, and for some sportsmen, race drivers, hang gliders, parachutists, the risk is an important part of the attraction.

How much greater a risk are we taking when we decide to fly off into the night with just one engine?

Let's analyze for a moment the kinds of risk to which we habitually expose ourselves. There are those, the automobile is a perfect example, in which the risk is largely due to the possible actions of others. The average driver, excluding race drivers, drag enthusiasts and other nuts who use a car for thrill purposes, is reasonably competent at handling his car and under normal circumstances is not likely to get into an accident, unless he is run into by someone else or unless some unforeseen happening—a kid or dog running into the street; a skid on a slippery road; another car unexpectedly swerving or braking—causes him to lose control. We accept these risks as we accept the common cold, unpleasant but an unavoidable fact of life.

Other types of risk are purely personal, involving just our-selves and no one else. If we want to smoke and take a chance of endangering our health, it's our business and not anyone else's. If we like to jump out of airplanes and watch the ground rushing at us before pulling the ripcord, we don't endanger anyone else and we can't blame anyone but ourselves if we get hurt or killed doing it.

A third kind of risk is the one we are taking when we entrust our lives and well being to the actions of others. When we take a taxi, we take it for granted that the driver is going to get us to our destination in one piece. When we step aboard an airliner, we assume that the pilot is competent and that the airplane isn't going to fall apart. When we go to a doctor or dentist we feel confident that he knows what he is doing.

Now back to night flying.

We freely admit that flying involves a calculated risk and that night flying in single-engine aircraft does increase this risk to a degree. To what degree depends on the individual pilot. What are the parameters with respect to weather which he has decided are acceptable for night flight? Does he own his own airplane and does he know from personal observation that whoever is doing the

How much of a risk are we taking when we decide to fly off into the night with just one engine?

maintenance is competent? Or, does he fly rented aircraft and, if so, what does he know of the condition of the airplane and the competency of the people who maintain it and, for that matter, the degree of care taken of it by the last pilots who flew it?

And about himself. How confident is he to be able to control an airplane entirely by instruments? How good are his eyes? How tired is he on the night for which the flight is planned? How competent is he with respect to using only the radios for navigation and, if it is a rented airplane, how familiar is he with the equipment in that particular airplane?

These and other questions should be the ones a pilot asks himself in determining the degree of risk to which he is about to expose himself, and only he himself can know whether the flight itself is sufficiently important to make that risk acceptable.

But what about his passengers. It's one thing for us to happily climb into an airplane and go scooring off into the dark. It's our butt. Period. Nobody else's. But passengers are another story. A non-pilot passenger, when he boards a light aircraft, may only be vaguely aware of whether it has one engine or two, and even if he is, it is doubtful that he is aware of the difference in terms of safety.

Furthermore, it must be assumed that he is confident of the pilot's competency, otherwise why would he have agreed to fly with him? Admittedly, there are recency-of-experience requirements, calling for so many night takeoffs and landings within a given period of time to let a pilot legally carry passengers at night. But who really pays attention to these rules? I'm sure that some pilots do, but I'm also sure that a lot of them don't.

I firmly believe that what is an acceptable set of conditions for a pilot flying alone, may not be acceptable when he takes on the responsibility for passengers. This tends to frequently put us in a quandry. The non-pilot passenger hasn't the faintest notion of the degree to which weather conditions can influence the safety of a flight. He knows only that airliner and all kinds of other airplanes are flying around in all kinds of weather, day and night, and he therefore simply assumes that everybody can do that. So, when he meets us at the airport, loaded with luggage and ready to go, it makes us feel kind of silly to have to tell him that, sorry, we can't go tonight; especially if, while we are saying this, we can hear another airplane taking off.

So maybe he thinks we are chicken. So what? Let him. Better a live chicken than a dead hero or a dead passenger or both. The trouble with passengers is, we know that we are taking a calculated risk, but do they?

Chapter 4

To File or Not to File

For those pilots who are not instrument rated the choice does not exist (legally, that is). For the instrument-rated pilot it's a different story. Basically, of course, flying instruments at night is no different from flying instruments in the daytime, regardless of whether the weather is VFR or IFR. The difference becomes important only in the event of an emergency.

As is explained elsewhere in these pages, the cautious night flyer will pick a reasonably high altitude, and will fly a modified zig-zag course which keeps him within reasonable distance of a lighted airport at all times. If you file an IFR flight plan, you can, of course, request the altitude you want to fly, but requesting a routing which hops, skips and jumps from one airport to another would be exceedingly cumbersome and would probably baffle the ATC computer as well as the controllers subsequently handling the flight. Not only is such type of flying impractical on an IFR flight plan, you also may find that you don't get the altitude you want because of conflicting traffic. (None of this is a consideration if you're flying a twin. Since the whole point of the precautions is to be able to get to an airport in case of engine trouble, any twin, even the most under-powered among the light-light twins, will be able to maintain a reasonable altitude long enough to get to an airport. Most of them won't climb with any degree of efficiency on one engine, and in the Rockies some may actually be incapable of maintaining a safe obstacle-clearance altitude with one fan feathered.)

What about, when the weather is, in fact, IFR? Obviously, a flight in IFR weather, regardless of night or day, can only be made by filing an IFR flight plan. Some pilots insist that single-engine IFR is too much of a risk at any time. They simply feel that in case of engine trouble, the single-engine pilot has too small a chance of coming down somewhere safely. Others habitually file, no matter whether the weather is good or bad. Neither is necessarily the right or the wrong way. It remains a matter of the pilot's personal preference.

What cannot be denied is that the calculated risk which we accept when flying single-engine aircraft at night or in IFR conditions, is multiplied when both are present at the same time. In daylight, when operating in IFR conditions, the pilot confronted with engine trouble can usually expect to break out of the clouds a sufficient distance above the ground to look for and find an acceptable place on which to make an emergency landing. At night that chance is reduced to next to nil. Only if such an emergency happened to develop over a well-lighted (and therefore well populated) area, could the pilot expect to drop down through the bottom of the clouds and see enough of the ground in order to put the bird down without killing himself (and his passengers) in the bargain.

We might point out here that landing in populated areas, though certainly not recommended, has been done successfully with considerable frequency. People have time and again landed on freeways, in schoolyards or on parking lots, and there is one instance on record where a pilot put down his single-engine Cessna on the George Washington Bridge without a scratch. (Subsequently a truck ran into the wing. Too bad.)

My personal preference with respect to night flying is to do it VFR and to stay in VFR conditions or on the ground. Admittedly, it hasn't always worked out that way, but that doesn't change the fact that it is what I like to strive for.

By the way at one time VFR night flying was not permitted in Mexico. And this brought about a rather funny situation when my son and I were in La Paz in Baja California and wanted to take off in mid-afternoon for a flight back to Los Angeles. We casually tried to fly from La Paz to Mexicali (as a stop there is mandatory before leaving Mexico), not knowing anything about that night-VFR restriction. This was in the early 1960s when neither of us were instrument rated. Well, we were told that we couldn't file to Mexicali because it would be night by the time our Comanche would get us there. The best they had to offer was a flight plan to Santa Rosalia (about half way), where we would then have to stay overnight and wait for daylight.

We grumbled a bit but then said, okay. So the fellow filled out all that paperwork which seems to be part and parcel of flying in Mexico. Then, when he handed it back to us he said in a sort of off-hand manner: "Of course, you may accidentally not be able to find Santa Roslia, in which case you'd have no choice but to go on to Mexicali."

It didn't take a great deal of ingenuity for us to at the right time look out of the wrong window and thus to "accidentally" miss Santa Rosalia. We landed at Mexicali and it took a bit of doing (and $5) to get some official to come out to the airport and to clear us out of the country. When he was all through, he informed us that, of course, we couldn't take off because it was after dark.

We pointed to the lights of Calexico, right across the border less than a mile distant, but he remained adamant. Then, just as he turned to leave, he said pointedly, "Of course, I'll be leaving now." And he did.

We took off without anyone trying to stop us and once approaching Calexico arranged to fly direct to Los Angeles International and to get our customs inspection there. Remember, this was in 1963, before the two countries were getting nervous about all that smuggling of marijuana. Today this might not have been that easy. I since have flown VFR at night in Mexico on one other occasion, and I frankly don't know whether the restrictions against VFR night flight are still in effect.

Chapter 5

Navigation at Night

Let's start off by saying that there are different kinds of nights. There are nights illuminated by a full moon, there are pitch black nights and there are those which fall somewhere in between. While even a full moon in a clear sky will not give sufficient light to permit us to make out terrain features in any meaningful detail, it does provide us with a degree of visual reference to the horizon or, in mountainous terrain, to the mountains which we want to stay away from.

Any pilot embarking on his first night flight would be well advised to pick a clear night when the moon is full. Somehow this is a gradual and more pleasant introduction to the vageries of night flying, than if he plunges into the ink-blackness of a moonless or overcast night.

One way or the other, though, it should be understood that night flying requires of the pilot the ability to control his aircraft by reference to instruments alone, and to navigate by whatever electronic navigation equipment he has in his airplane, even though he is operating technically VFR.

But that shouldn't be interpreted as meaning that pilotage is of no use. Quite the contrary. If the weather is clear and the visibility reasonably decent, we can see for miles ahead and we should use this ability by cross-checking what we see with what our nav radios tell us. After all, if we planned our flight correctly, it will, in fact, consist of relatively short straight legs from one lighted city with a lighted airport to the next. Between these cities and towns are

There are nights illuminated by the moon...

highways and, regardless of the time of night, there are always cars and trucks to show us the way.

If we thus keep ourselves occupied by checking these cities, roads and other visible features against the Sectionals (or WACs) it will serve a dual purpose. One, we will never be in doubt as to our present position. Two, we'll be busy and thus find it easier to stay awake.

Until it has happened a few times it is hard to accept how easy it is to get lost at night. Time seems to pass more slowly and we keep thinking that we should be farther along than we actually are. So we suddenly find that we are convinced that that town we are looking at is one which is actually still 50 miles distant. (I remember once circling over Dalhart, Texas, happily convinced that it was Amarillo, simply because I had failed to keep track of my ground speed and had, apparently, picked up a healthy headwind somewhere along the way.) A constant awareness of what ground speed is being made good is one great help in avoiding this kind of confusion.

There are, of course, different kinds of being lost. One kind which happens to all of us in the daytime as well as at night, is knowing that we are generally on course, but not knowing exactly where on it. It's the old story of a passenger asking the pilot, "Where are we?" And the pilot answering, "Oh, I don't know. Somewhere between here and there."

Good practice, at night, is to periodically, say, every 15 or 20 minutes, tune in some off-course VOR and determine the exact position of the aircraft on the course being flown. It keeps us aware of changes in ground speed and avoids those nasty surprises caused by sudden fluctuations in wind direction and velocity.

The other kind of lost is being really lost, meaning that we have let ourselves drift off course and we suddenly become aware that neither the nav-receiver indications nor what we are able to see by looking out of the window are what they should be if we were where we thought we were.

Don't panic. The first reaction should be a look at the fuel gauges. How much time do we have before diminishing fuel becomes a factor? Since it should be a hard and fast rule that we should never remain airborne at night with less than an hour's fuel on board, we should have at least that much. Okay, so, unless we are under an overcast, we climb up to 10,000 or 12,000 feet and play with the OBS and nav receiver until we pick up some reliable needle reaction in the OBI. Unless we have been thoroughly inattentive for a very long time, we should have some idea of the general area in which we are scooting around, and should therefore be able to check the appropriate VOR frequencies for stations within reasonable distance on whatever chart we are using. Since it is virtually impossible to be in the air at that altitude anywhere over the contiguous 48 states without being also within reception distance of at least one VOR, it should be possible to figure out the present position.

But if that doesn't work or if, because of overcast conditions, we can't climb high enough to pick up any of the VORs we think are appropriate, the next step should be to tune to com radio to any of the VOR simplex communication frequencies (122.2; 122.3; 123.6; 123.65) and call blind, asking any station receiving the call to please respond. If one frequency brings no answer, try the next, and the next. Then if all else fails, we might try the emergency frequency (121.5) which is supposed to be monitored by most ATC facilities, or we might try and call the ARTCC by picking the frequency for the center sector which looks like the one for the area in which we believe ourselves to be.

Once contact has been established, the thing to do is to own up and admit we're lost. There are any number of means by which ATC can locate us and, unless we have waited too long and are running out of fuel, guide us safely to an airport.

A case in point happened in Southern California. A pilot (with passengers) had taken off from Los Angeles on a flight to San Francisco. The weather was reasonably clear inland, but the coast

Clouds frequently obscure mountaintops.

was obscured by low clouds and fog. How he managed it nobody will ever know, but somehow he must have flown for a rather long time without paying any attention to his nav instruments, because when he finally contacted Santa Barbara Radio, admitting that he had no idea where he was, they, using DF, found him 60 miles off the coast over the ocean. They tried to guide him to the nearest VFR airport, but he had apparently waited too long, because he ran out of fuel before reaching land and crashing, killing himself and all on board.

During night flight certain types of terrain can become a disconcerting factor. Large bodies of water, for instance, like the Great Lakes or the Long Island Sound turn into featureless blackness which, while harmless in itself, does tend to make us nervous. As much as we may dislike the idea of flying long detours as would be necessary if, for instance, on a flight from Grand Rapids to Milwaukee we wanted to stay within sight (and gliding distance) of land, it should be seriously considered, unless we are quite certain that the prolonged lack of any visual features won't cause us to get panicky.

Flying the Rockies at night is another experience in which ground features can get kind of spooky. Since the mountains in certain portions stick up to over 14,000 feet, there are bound to be times when we'll be flying at an altitude below the highest elevation of such rocks. In addition, populated areas are few and far between and VORs are scarce.

35

On such a flight it would not be at all unusual to be flying away from a VOR above a valley lined on both sides by high mountains. If there is a good-sized moon, we'll be able to see the mountains and as a result navigating is not too difficult. If, on the other hand, it is one of those black moonless nights, it may be totally impossible to see the mountains. In that case the thing to do is to establish the exact VOR radial that leads down the valley and stays clear of the mountains, and then fly along it, keeping the needle meticulously centered at all times.

On a night like that, when in doubt, it would be better to climb to an altitude which assures us that we are well above any terrain features in the vicinity, than to take chances at a lower altitude.

On nights when the sky is obscured by clouds, flying in the mountains is next to suicidal. Clouds frequently obscure mountain tops and might force us to meander around in the pitch dark below where VOR reception can easily be lost because of interfering terrain. Caught in a situation like that, the best action would be to pick up a well-traveled highway and follow it to the nearest town with an airport. Mountain flying is tough enough in the daytime. Night only makes it worse.

In summary, then, the best advice that can be given to the night flyer with regard to navigation is to constantly pay attention. Navigating itself is not much more difficult than it is in the daytime. What is more difficult is to try and extricate oneself from a situation caused by sloppy flying or lack of awareness of changing wind and other conditions which affect groundspeed, heading and range. Don't start off a night-flying career by taking off from, say, Los Angeles at four or five in the afternoon with St. Louis as destination and Albuquerque as a fuel stop. Rather take it easy at first. An hour or two on a bright moonlit night in an an area where the terrain and airports are familiar. Get used to what it feels like and looks like before planning multi-hundred-mile cross-countries.

Chapter 6
The Anatomy of a Night Flight

It is, of course, supposed to be an inviolate rule that, before embarking on any flight, we make all kinds of preparations: Analyze our route of flight, check weather and winds, determine the fuel stops en route, if any, figure out the most advantageous altitude at which to fly and, if we really want to be thorough, make up a written flight log with radials and bearings to be flown and listing the various frequencies which we will be using along our route. Well, quite frankly, once we get past the initial few hundred hours, much of this becomes theory. What we tend to do in practice is to go out to the airport, look up at the sky, then look the airplane over to make sure that nothing untoward is hanging or dripping. We then simply climb in, head in the general direction in which we know we want to go, and after a while pick up the radio and get that weather briefing that we didn't bother with before takeoff. As one pilot likes to say with a crooked grin: "What's the point of checking the weather? You might find out you can't go."

Then, as the flight progresses we gradually find an altitude that appeals to us and after a while we glance at the charts to figure out what might be a good place to stop for fuel and, maybe, a cup of coffee. Of course, we also use our charts, which may or may not be current, to check on the appropriate VOR frequencies, but generally it's all a very casual process, because after all, 99 percent of the time there isn't much to it.

That's all very nice in the daytime, but at night it just won't do. For most of us night flights follow a day, often a long day, of business

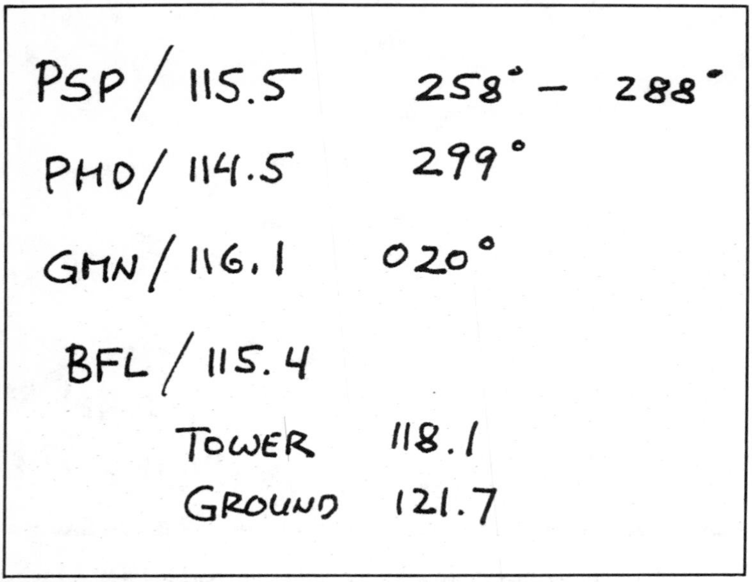

PSP / 115.5   258° — 288°

PHO / 114.5   299°

GMN / 116.1   020°

BFL / 115.4

    TOWER   118.1

    GROUND   121.7

It is definitely a good idea to list the en-route frequencies on a separate piece of paper.

and work, and by the time we finally get ready to take off, we may think we are wide awake and as sharp as ever, but the actual fact is that much of the time we are operating on a diminishing amount of nervous energy. It therefore behooves us to do everyting we can to make the flight as uncomplicated as possible.

This means a fair amount of preparation. First, it goes without saying that we should forego the martini or scotch before dinner and the brandy after it. It might also be a good idea to cut down on the amount of smoking and to limit the dinner to a light one as the heavy feeling after a full-course meal adds to the body's tendency toward sleepiness.

Aside from these basic considerations, the next step is to drag out the charts and check our route of flight. The temptation, of course, is to plot a straight line as it promises the shortest flight time and the greatest fuel economy. But, especially when flying a single-engine aircraft, the smart thing to do is to fly a route which offers the best chance of being within sight (and possibly gliding distance) of a lighted airport all or most of the time, even if that means flying a number of doglegs.

In much of the country, when flying at about 8,000 or 10,000 feet, it is possible to keep at least one airport in sight, a reassuring feeling, to say the least. And for this very reason, when at all possible, night flights should be conducted at altitudes higher than those at which we normally like to operate. Even on westerly flights this should not pose any major problem as winds at night are usually not very strong, thus there should be no excessive headwind.

It is definitely a good idea to list the en-route VOR frequencies on a separate piece of paper, written with a pen with a fat point in black, so that they can easily be read in the lousy light available in most cockpits. It's a real drag to try and find a frequency on a chart in flight, even with the help of a flashlight and a magnifying glass.

The next step involves a firm decision as to where to stop for fuel. Many medium-sized and small airports either have no fuel service available at all after a certain hour, or getting service involves making a phone call after landing and then waiting for a disgruntled FBO to climb out of bed, get dressed and drive to the airport. So, fuel stops should be major cities with 24-hour service.

At this point, with a clear picture in mind of how far we want to go and what route we want to follow, let's call and check the weather. If it's CAVU all the way and the forecast upper winds are either favorable or light and variable, we're in luck. If patches of scattered or broken clouds are reported with bases at or below the level at which we want to fly, we may still be all right, but it would be a good idea to get a clear picture or exactly how far this cloudiness does extend, and we might want to ask for any available reports on

If scattered or broken clouds are reported we may want to ask for reports on the tops.

Okay, now it's time to take off.

the tops. We also want to make sure that the airport we have selected for a fuel stop is forecast to remain comfortably VFR. If there is any doubt it might be the better part of valor to opt for an alternate, not farther away but closer in. The reason to look for a closer one is that we don't ever want to run low on fuel at night. If we consider 45 minutes or even 30 minutes an adequate reserve during daylight, at night this figure should be doubled. Ample fuel is the most important safety feature available to the pilot. Ample reserves must be considered sacred.

If the forecast calls for broken or overcast clouds along all or much of the route, the primary question must be about ceilings and, if they are ample, are they expected to remain at that level or is there a chance that they lower later on? If the ceilings are amply high, say 10,000 feet or better, then they present no serious problem except that we can expect it to be about as dark as dark can get. (The extreme darkness surrounding an airplane at night cannot be emphasized enough for the novice pilot, accustomed to driving his car at night with headlights illuminating what lies ahead. In the air nothing lies ahead—it better not—and even if we did want to fly with our landing lights on, they wouldn't pick up a thing. The pure fact is, it's simply goddamn dark.)

If rain showers or thunderstorms are predicted for our route of flight, we might want to call the nearest motel and forget about the whole thing. Oh, it may be possible to make the flight just the same, but it can get pretty creepy, so, unless we are very experienced in flying at night (and if we are, why are we reading this book?), let's try and not get involved in any real weather.

All right, assuming conditions are adequate, we decide to go. Even though VFR flight plans are not mandatory and are of absolutely no advantage to anyone if everything goes according to Hoyle, it might be a good idea to file one anyway. If for some unforseen reason something does go wrong, at least somebody is going to have a fair idea where to start looking for us.

Okay, now it's time to take off. Let's make sure we have the charts we need, and if we habitually fly with Jeppesens, it would be advisable to carry a set of Sectionals along. Knowing where roads lead and knowing the approximate shape of towns and cities can be a great help. Do we have a flashlight with fresh batteries? Next to fuel and a wide-awake pilot, a flashlight can be the most important piece of equipment on a night flight. Many of us use glasses when reading in poor or artificial light, though we don't need them under normal conditions. Have your glasses handy, you will need them. Also a small magnifying glass is a good idea. A night cockpit is a lousy place to try and read all that fine print, and a magnifying glass can be a great help.

One more thing before firing up the engine. Are we at a familiar airport where we know where obstructions, high buildings, broad-

Do we know the location of obstructions in the vicinity of the airport?

cast towers, mountains, are located? If not, let's take one more look at the Sectional and memorize the location and height of obstructions. Once in the air it's a bit late to start to worry whether we'll make it across that mountain that is hidden out there somewhere in the blackness.

A thorough preflight is always a good idea, and at night it's even more so. Don't leave simple things to chance. Use the flashlight to check fuel and oil and to make sure that pitot covers have been removed and that all tiedown ropes are off and that no stray chocks are strewn around the ramp in front of the airplane.

TAXI

Keep the landing or taxi lights on while taxiing to the active runway. Not only does it help ground control (at a controlled airport) to keep track of the airplane, it also prevents you from accidentally running into some piece of junk, a cardboard box that has blown out onto the ramp or taxiway, a ladder left by some forgetful lineboy, or even a stray dog in search of some after-dark entertainment.

RUNUP

Don't be in a hurry. Perform a complete runup, exercise the prop and flaps, and, if you are taking off from a high-altitude airport, lean the mixture to about 100 degrees on the rich side of peak (while running the engine rather hard) to preclude an unexpected loss of power after takeoff because of excessively rich mixture or fouled plugs.

TAKEOFF

The takeoff should be strictly routine, except that you might want to monitor airspeed and the VSI somewhat more closely than normal, because in the darkness it is hard to visually judge the climb angle of the airplane and we don't want to take a chance of stalling while still close to the ground. (While it is virtually impossible to land on an unlighted airport, it is usually possible to take off from one. It's an uncomfortable feeling, much like taking off in zero-zero conditions, but there is usually enough light to permit us to line ourselves up with the runway and it is then simply a matter of maintaining the runway direction during acceleration and lift-off without wavering to one side or the other.)

CLIMB-OUT

During climb-out we generally lose all ground reference ahead of the airplane. We can, of course, look out of the window by our side if we feel that we want to make sure that the ground is still there, but in the direction in which we are flying, all we see are stars or, in case of an overcast sky, nothing at all. Though technically VFR, we are now, in fact, on instruments and except for looking out for other traffic (which is a lot easier to see at night than in the daytime) we should be flying by airspeed, artificial horizon, turn-and-bank, VSI, and the altimeter. This is true of much night flying and the pilot should feel confident that he can handle himself and the airplane by reference to instruments alone. If he can't, he has no business being up there after sunset.

Since it feels more comfortable to have some sort of ground reference ahead of the airplane, most pilots will prefer to cruise-climb in a fairly level attitude, once sufficient altitude has been achieved to clear any and all obstacles in the vicinity. By ground reference we primarily mean the lights from streets, automobiles, houses. Except on very bright full-moon nights, the ground itself will remain invisible, but no matter where we fly, there is always some insomniac driving his car and piercing the night with his headlights.

CRUISE

Once level at our altitude, preferably some eight or more thousand feet above the ground, we should keep on looking for the

Keep your taxi lights on when taxiing on an airport at night.

various airports along which we have plotted our route. Often, in the jumble of city lights, they are somewhat hard to find, but with a bit of practice we learn to glance from side to side and to pick up the tell-tale green-and-white beacons or the rows of parallel lights which, unlike roads, are ruler straight and lead nowhere.

On clear but moonless nights it is frequently hard to tell whether a light in the distance ahead is, in fact, a house or other light on the ground, or rather a star fairly close to the horizon. It doesn't particularly matter if we pay attention to the instruments, but we shouldn't let ourselves get fascinated by it. Forget it. If it moves it's a car. If it seems to be coming closer it's a fixed light on the ground. If it neither moves nor comes closer, it's a star.

Always be on the lookout for lights which suddenly disappear. If you've been flying toward a patch of lights in the distance ahead and suddenly it isn't there anymore, the only possible explanation is that something has crept between you and those lights. If you are flying low it could be a hill and you better start climbing fast. If you're high (as you should be), it's most likely a cloud. It could be an isolated little cloud of no particular consequence, but then again, it could be the beginning of a whole bunch of clouds, forcing you to decide whether to climb up over the top, to drop down below or to turn around and land somewhere.

Clouds, if they can be seen at all, vary in appearance and can be deceiving. In the vicinity of brightly lit cities they tend to appear grey on the underside and darker on top. In moonlight they are grey on top and dark on the bottom. In the kind of haze conditions which frequently cover the better part of the East and Midwest, clouds may appear as dark shapes in a slightly lighter soup-like surrounding. There are no hard and fast rules and the only sure way to know that you've flown into a cloud is the sudden eery red and green glow from your wingtip navigation lights.

When flying in a cloud (don't, unless you're IFR) or in severe haze conditions, you may want to turn off the rotating beacon or strobes, as their rhythmic illumination has a mesmerizing effect and can result in vertigo.

Generally, cruising at night is quite lovely. Most of the time the air is smooth, the winds minimal, and there is a sort of peacefulness about it that one rarely experiences during the daytime. But, especially if you've got the autopilot turned on, it's also inducive to falling asleep. There are a number of tricks to help us stay awake. One is to turn off the autopilot and hand-fly the airplane. But, especially in smooth air, that may not do much good since, as we all know, modern airplanes are sufficiently stable to need very little help from the pilot to stay straight and level. Another good thing to do is to talk to as many FSSs as are available. Talking somehow helps. If that becomes too monotonous, turn on the ADF and listen to music, the louder and more raucous, the better. Also, wiggle your toes, sing on the top of your voice, cut down the heater and open a vent or two. Set yourself tasks, such as trying to estimate the time of the next checkpoint or some such. And, for heaven's sake, don't close your

At night clouds tend to vary in appearance and can be deceiving.

eyes just to rest them for a moment. You may just forget to open them again.

There is one trick for the really tired pilot flying on the autopilot. Lock it onto the nearest VOR. All except the most sophisticated and expensive autopilots cause the airplane to bank one way and then the other quite rapidly when overflying a VOR, and unless you are an exceptionally sound sleeper, that should be enough to wake you up. And when it does it is likely to be such a shock, that your adrenelin starts flowing like mad, causing you to be wide awake from then on.

Certain weather conditions, though technically VFR, can make night flight a literal nightmare. One such is haze. You climb and climb and climb and above you there are the stars and possibly the moon. But all around you there is some sort of milky soup obscuring the horizon and most if not all of the ground below. Eventually you've got to stop climbing because you've reached oxygen altitudes and there is no oxygen on board. Thick haze like that (dust storms are just as bad) have a disorienting effect on all but the experienced instrument pilot. It becomes absolutely necessary to monitor the instruments and to religiously believe in what they show, no matter if the so-called seat of the pants insists on arguing that they are wrong. The seat of the pants or, more scientifically, the inner ear, is a liar. Drop a wing and fly at a bank for a few moments, and you inner ear will insist that you're flying straight and level. Then, when you pick up the wing and fly straight again, it will try and persuade you that you are actually in an opposite bank. Tell it to shut up and trust the instruments. They're the only uncorruptible reference you've got.

Flying in VFR conditions on top of a solid overcast always has its elements of suspense. Is the overcast going to stop before we get to where we want to go? Are the tops going to stay where they are or are they going to start to rise to an uncomfortable degree? Are we going to be able to find a hole to drop down through just in case it doesn't stop by the time we want to land? In the daytime the visibility up there is usually pretty good and we can see for miles, and with a bit of experience we can learn to judge the composition of the undercast, even from quite a ways away. At night, no such luck. The light of the moon (if any) and the stars will paint some sort of image of the clouds below us, sufficient to keep us from dropping down into them without being aware of it. But most of the time it is impossible to tell whether the tops of the clouds ahead are remaining at the same level, are rising or lowering. The only way we have to find out the extent of the cloud cover is to call an FSS and ask for

Flying in VFR conditions on top of a solid overcast always has its elements of suspense.

weather conditions in various directions, hoping to find one within range that is reporting clear, scattered or even broken conditions.

Breaks in the overcast are of absolutely no use unless they happen to be over a town or a heavily travelled road providing enough light to see the extent of the hole and get a reasonably clear picture of the ground below. And even then we better have prior information about the height of the ceiling, because we don't want to find ourselves below a low overcast miles from the nearest airport, forced to fly along highways or something at an altitude at which chimneys and broadcast towers represent an ever present danger.

Unless an overcast is immensely thick, the locations of cities and towns can be spotted as more or less pie-shaped milky spots, but, except for giving us the satisfaction of proving that we are still on course (we hope), those light areas are of absolutely no value to us.

As a general rule, if there is a large area of solid overcast between us and our destination, we would probably be a lot better off to either stay below, assuming the ceiling is sufficient to permit flight at a safe obstruction-clearance altitude, or to give up the flight altogether and go to sleep in order to fly again in the morning.

THUNDERSTORMS

They can present a fascinating spectacle at night, and at least they have the decency to provide their own illumination. Actually, because of the lightning which paints brief but extremely clear pictures of the cloud formations surrounding the storm, thunderstorms are easily avoided. If it's an isolated storm, flying around it may use up time and fuel, but otherwise is quite easy. If it's a whole squall line with one storm next to the other, the problem is the same as it would be in the daytime. Don't! Turn around, land and wait. It's just not very bright to hope to find a safe place to get through. And remember, if you goof, your airplane is no match for one of those beasts.

RAIN

Except for the fact that most lightplane cockpits tend to leak, rain itself is nothing much to worry about. It sounds frightening and, if you momentarily turn on your landing light, it looks worse—like a million machinegun bullets coming straight at you—but with night visibility being nothing to write home about under the best of conditions, the reduction in visibility because of the rain doesn't make that much difference. You might want to turn on your carburetor heat (unless you're flying a fuel-injected engine) just to play safe, because chances are that with all that moisture you might just pick up carburetor ice, but aside from that, just keep on trucking, as they say. It'll probably stop sooner or later.

In other chapters in this book we'll be using the examples of specific (mostly actual) flights to illustrate some of the problems facing the night flyer, so let's just assume that on this particular occasion the destination is clear and we end this chapter with one of those perfect greased-on landings that all of us dream about.

Chapter 7
The Night Landing

All right, so we have managed to successfully navigate to our destination, and now, right there over the nose of the airplane, is the friendly green and white rotating beacon of the airport. Let's say it's an airport that has a 24-hour control tower. So we call, announce ourselves, and, in turn, receive the usual information: Temperature, altitmeter setting, wind, runway in use, and so on. We also know, or at least should know the airport elevation and, in turn, the number of feet we have to come down from our present altitude. As we get closer we see the runway lights and, using them as guide, we can align ourselves to the runway, either on a downwind leg or for a straight-in approach, depending on the directions received from the tower. During this phase it is of considerable importance to know the airport elevation and to be sure that the altimeter is set to the current altimeter information applicable to the airport because, unlike in daylight, it is very difficult indeed to judge our altitude by some sort of visual reference. If the two rows of runway lights were spaced the same distance apart at all airports, it would be a relatively simple matter to gain experience as to what they should look like when viewed from a given altitude. But they are not; and when they are placed far apart we tend to think we are lower than we actually are, while others, placed close to the edges of a fairly narrow runway, will make us think that we're much too high.

While obstructions in the vicinity of airports are often identified by red obstruction lights, one should never depend on that. It is therefore a matter of simple logic to stay high and make a fairly steep final approach to touchdown. Long, low, drag-it-in approaches, though not particularly intelligent at any time (what a depressing experience it would be to lose power on final and tear the gear off just 50 feet short of the threshold), at night are to be avoided at all cost. An unlighted cow or a parked car or even just a high fence would be impossible to see until it's too late. So let's keep it higher than we might in the daytime and, if necessary, slip off some altitude once we know that we've got the runway made.

At uncontrolled airports there are some additional precautions that should be taken. First of all, let's make sure it is really the airport we're after. It's awfully easy at night to spot a lighted airport in the general area where we think it should be, and then to simply decide that this must be it. Always double-check the VOR readings, because nothing is quite as embarrassing as to land and then to find out that the place you really wanted to be is another 10 miles down the road.

Once we're sure that that's where we want to go, overfly the airport and look for the tetrahendron or windsock. Just because the wind aloft was clearly out of the west, doesn't mean it's going to be blowing in the same direction at ground level. It's amazing how difficult it can be, at times, to read those indications from the air at night, and sometimes it takes three or four turns around the airport to make sure we're got the wind direction right.

Then fly a precise and standard pattern. When it's quite obvious that the airport is half asleep and there isn't any traffic within miles, it is tempting to ignore the pattern and just make any kind of an approach that promises to be the least time consuming. Forget it! It's tough enough to make a descent landing when all one can see of the ground are two rows of lights. Flying a complete standard pattern with a fairly steep final approach reduces guesswork to a minimum and offers the best chance of a good landing.

Landing at night at a big major terminal can be a confusing experience. Since winds at night are generally not too strong, quite frequently more than one runway is in use at the same time and, therefore, has its runway lights on. So, the first thing, after being told by the tower the active runway, is to figure out which one is which. That's fairly simple if they are at more or less right angles to one another, but if, as is the case at Love Field in Dallas, for instance, we're talking about Runway 15 and Runway 18, getting ourselves lined up to the wrong runway is an easy matter. Usually, unless the tower is very busy, he'll call us and embarass us by telling us that we're lined up with the wrong runway, but at other times we may find ourselves on final, possibly in conflict with another airplane,

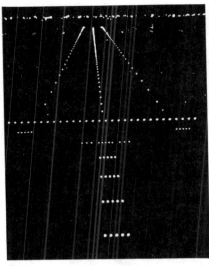

Are you sure that this is the runway to which you were cleared?

before realizing our mistake. So let's make sure to check the DG early in the game so that there can be no doubt about the exact direction of the runway we're looking for.

Another problem, also present during daytime but compounded at night, is avoiding wake turbulence when following a landing jet. In the daytime it's easy to spot his touchdown point and then make sure to land beyond it. At night that is more difficult but not less important. Not only is it hard to tell exactly when his wheels touch the ground (at which point wake turbulence is no longer generated), but it is also difficult to judge the particular spot on the runway. The best advice is, since most jet runways are quite long, to land about halfway down the runway. That should leave plenty of room for the average light plane to come to a complete stop far short of the end of the runway, while it offers relatively certain assurance that the jet touched down before that point.

Then, of course, comes that messy business of trying to make sense out of that bewildering array of blue lights which are supposed to help us find the taxiways. Don't try and look too far ahead. The only way to use those lights is to pay attention to the ones right in front of you and to stay between the rows. Farther in the distance they turn into a hopeless jumble that doesn't seem to make any sort of sense.

Do keep you landing light or taxi light on while taxiing. They don't do much good in telling you where to go, but they do help to spot sudden obstructions. A very drastic example of this was brought home to me one night when, after landing at Boston's Logan

Then comes that messy business of trying to make sense out of that bewildering array of blue lights which are supposed to help us find the taxiways.

Airport, I was taxiing to the ramp. Suddenly, there right in front of me in the middle of the taxiway stood an aluminum ladder. If I hadn't had my taxi lights on I might have ended up with a two-thousand-dollar propeller repair bill. On the other hand, if there is a line attendant motioning you into a tiedown space, it is only polite to turn those lights off as they tend to be most annoying to someone facing the airplane.

As we all know, flying an airplane several thousand feet above the ground in reasonably good weather is a lead-pipe cinch. The knowing where you are and getting where you want to go without getting seriously lost along the way, is also not the most difficult thing in the world. As a matter of fact, if we never had to land, flying would be the nearest thing to child's play. It's that inescapable need to eventually get back on the ground that tends to give aviation a bad name. Somehow, *terra firma* and airplanes don't mix too well, and that is especially true at night. For this reason it is advisable that a pilot, embarking on a night flight, think realistically about how tired he is likely to be when the time comes for him to put the damn thing down. Night is a time for sleep, and it is not illogical to assume that a pilot taking off at dusk for a three or four hour flight has probably been up since early morning and working all day, meaning that by midnight or two or three in the morning, he is not as sharp as he might have been some five or six hours earlier. The reports of pilots

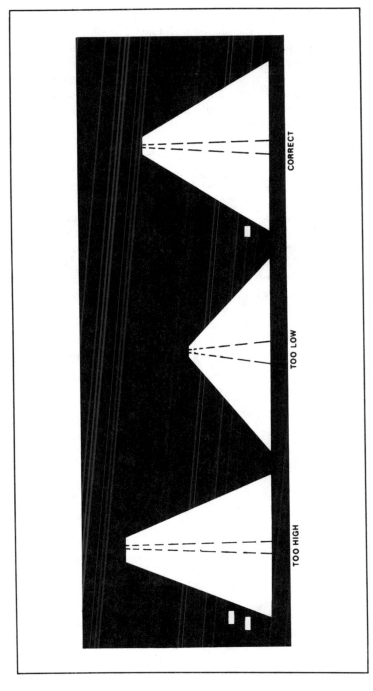

VASI landing aids can be found at many airports.

taking off in the evening, putting the airplane on autopilot, and then, fast asleep, flying into the side of a mountain, are legion.

One good way to sharpen the reflexes prior to the chore of landing, is to disconnect the autopilot some 100 miles or at least a half an hour before arriving at the destination airport. Hand-flying the airplane tends to get our adrenelin going, meaning that the lethargy produced by prolonged flight is reduced to a minimum and our senses are being somewhat sharpened by the simple expedient of manually handling the controls.

In recent years a very efficient landing aid, called VASI (for visual approach slope indicator) has been installed at the approach end of the most frequently used runways at many airports. It consists of two rows of lights positioned on either side of the runway. These lights will appear white when the aircraft is above the accepted glide-slope angle, they appear red when it is below that glide path and appear red at the top and white at the bottom during a normal approach. VASIs are normally operative during day as well as night and are most helpful in eliminating the confusion which can result when a runway is either much wider or much narrower than normal.

By carefully monitoring the VASI indications any reasonably efficient pilot can't help but make the right approach and, as is obvious, any flight that culminates in a successful landing is a safe flight.

Chapter 8
Charts

Let's spend a few moments analyzing the aviation charts and their usefulness when flying at night. For all practical purposes there are three types of charts which we habitually use: The Sectionals, printed in a scale of 1:500,000; the WAC charts, printed in a scale of 1:1,000,000; and the Low-Altitude En-Route charts which come in two versions, those issued by the government and those produced and marketed by Jeppesen. They are printed in scales varying from 10 nm per inch to 30 nm per inch.

When we first start to fly we usually use the Sectionals, as they seem to be the easiest to read. But then, after a while, many of us get tired of lugging all that paper around with us, and we might switch to the WAC charts which show more than twice the area on the same amount of paper. Then, either because we start working on our instrument rating, or simply because it just seems more professional, we may decide to switch to Jeppesens. They use up even less space, are easy to read (once one gets the hang of them) and are ideal for navigating strictly by the VORs.

What do they show?

SECTIONALS

On the front and back covers they show which part of the country is represented by the particular chart. They print all the symbols used on the chart with explanations of what they all mean. And they show the highest elevation and its location. On the face of the chart itself we find the locations of cities, towns and villages, represented in a shape which fairly accurately represents what these places look like from the air. An immense amount of topographical information is included: Mountains, valleys, rivers; and man-made features such as highways, high towers, pipelines, high-tension lines, railroads, and anything else that can easily be seen from the air. They show the exact location of airports with an approximation of the runway layout and an indication whether the airport is controlled or uncontrolled, whether it is lighted, has a rotating beacon, the airport elevation, longest runway and so on. All VORs are clearly shown with their usable frequencies, as are NDBs and the more useful standard broadcast stations. And then there are the Victor Airways, the outlines of various types of controlled and uncontrolled airspace (not a particularly useful feature), and prohibited, restricted and warning areas with information about the controlling agency and how to contact it. Also indicated are the applicable ARTCCs and their sectors, plus a listing of their frequencies.

There is more, such as state borders, the extent of the various time zones, lines of magnetic variation, warnings about magnetic disturbances, wildlife refuges and wilderness areas. In other words, the charts provide a literally staggering amount of information, and their only drawback really is that they are rather large, approximately two by five feet, and therefore a bit unwieldy in the cockpit.

WAC

While Sectionals are available only for the 48 contiguous United States, VAC (World Aeronautical Charts) charts cover the U.S., Hawaii and Alaska, Mexico, Central America (and comparable charts are available for the rest of the world in the same scale). For all practical purposes WAC charts contain the same information as the Sectionals, except, since more than twice the area is represented on an equal size charts, the information tends to get rather crowded and, therefore, hard to read. Since they are just as big as the Sectionals, they, too, are cumbersome in the cockpit, but while it takes 36 Sectionals to cover the lower 48 states, it only takes 11 WACs. The choice between the two is a matter of pilot preference (and eyesight). Personally, I like the Sectionals better for reasons which I'll be explaining later in this chapter.

LOW ALTITUDE EN ROUTE CHARTS

These charts, whether we're talking about Jeppesens or those issued by the government, are, in fact, radio-facility charts. This means that they show nav aids, the Victor Airway network, distances between VORs, intersections, MEAs, MRAs, MOCAs, frequencies, the location of most (but not all) airports. They do not show cities and towns, rivers, roads, mountains or other terrain features (though the Jeppesens do include indications of major lakes, coast lines and such). They make radio navigation easy but are totally useless for finding our way by any other means. The choice between Jeppesens and the government charts is, again, a matter of personal preference. I like Jeppesens because I find them easier to read and they do seem to contain somewhat more information.

When flying at night, unable to see what the terrain below looks like, the conscientious pilot should have charts on board which give him that information. In other words, he should have the applicable Sectionals or WACs, even if he prefers to do most or all of his navigating by his Jeppesens. There are a number of reasons. One, if his radios, or even just his nav reciever(s) should, for one reason or another, fail to function, he can at least continue to navigate using cities and roads as a guide; but for this he has to know the shape of those cities or towns and the direction and configuration of the roads. This is quite feasible with Sectionals but much more difficult with WACs, because the needed information is just too small and, in an ill-lit cockpit using a flashlight, too difficult to reliably identify.

Another need for Sectionals could arise if a lowering overcast forces the pilot down onto the deck. Not only is the VOR reception distance reduced to a point where the pilot might be out of contact with any nav aid for some time, but it is also important for him to be aware of high broadcast towers and other obstructions which, though supposedly equipped with obstruction lights, are often hard to see, especially if there are haze conditions or it's raining.

What must be remembered when using Sectionals or WACs in the cockpit at night, is that much of the information is printed in shades of red and tends to disappear if viewed in the red light of the average cockpit illumination. When using these charts, always turn on some white light source, either the dome light or a flashlight or, of course, a map light if the aircraft is so equipped.

My own preference for night flight is to use Jeppesens and to have a set of Sectionals available as a backup.

Chapter 9
Instruments

The instruments necessary for safe and efficient night flight are really not much different than those needed to fly in the daytime. If there is a difference, it is that we can get away with a lot less instrumentation in the daytime than we can at night.

While few of us may want to do it, it is perfectly possible to fly a lengthy daytime cross-country without any radios at all, using just our compass, altimeter and airspeed indicater, while looking out of the window to keep track of where we are and where we are going.

Looking out of the window at night doesn't work too well. Sure, unless we're above an overcast, we can see and possibly recognize some towns and roads, but efficient navigation by pure pilotage is next to impossible for any length of time. In other words, the availability of one (or preferably two) nav receivers is an absolute necessity. The fact is that night flight should be considered instrument flying in all aspects except that we don't file IFR and do not maintain contact with ATC.

Of course, having those radios on board is not enough. We also have to know how to use them, and anyone not thoroughly comfortable with them would be a lot better advised to land somewhere before the sun goes down.

There is one important difference in the way our VOR receiver should be used at night. During daylight hours (when VFR) we habitually tune in a station without bothering to make sure that the station we are receiving is actually the one we want. After all, we can see that the needle indication is as expected with reference to features on the ground. At night it should be considered an absolute must to listen to the station identifier before acting upon the signal that is being received. It is amazing how quickly one can find oneself miles off course as the result of only momentary inattention.

An ADF is another nice instrument to have around, but unlike the VOR receiver, it must be treated somewhat differently at night than in the day. ADFs are subject to something called "night effect" which requires a bit of explanation. Radio waves in the low-frequency bands (the ones used by the ADF) have a way of spilling out into the atmosphere and then being bounced back to earth as they hit the ionosphere. But the ionosphere doesn't act like a smooth mirror. It is bumpy and uneven and tends to deflect the waves in an unpredictable manner. As a result, the ADF needle tends to fluctuate from one side to the other and a pilot, using it for navigation, should not try to follow each fluctuation but rather split the difference and fly the average of the various directions being indicated. This aberration doesn't happen to any noticeable degree in the daytime. It is at its worst around sunset and sunrise, and persists to some degree throughout the night. It is most noticeable when we are tuned to a station with a higher rather than low kHz number. So whenever possible, the station with the lowest frequency should be selected.

Here, too, it is important to reliably identify the station we believe to have tuned to. If it's an NDB, LOM or other navigational facility, listen to the station's audio identifier before switching to the nav mode. If we are trying to use a standard broadcast station for navigation, this is more complicated because these stations don't bother to identify themselves with any frequency. And, at night, we sometimes receive stations located hundreds of miles distant without realizing it. Once, flying between Phoenix and Los Angeles at night, I listened for a long time to a station which turned out to be located in Philadelphia, Pennsylvania, of all places.

A word of warning about navigating toward an LOM. LOMs are used by ATC to guide instrument traffic toward the airport at which they are located. That means that chances are that a fair amount of jet traffic will overfly the LOM at a fairly low altitude in the process of making an instrument approach. VFR traffic not in contact with ATC would always do better to stay away from these instrument-approach lanes as heavy jet aircraft, flying slow with flaps down and high-lift devices deployed, are unable to take sudden evasive action, and, after all, who wants to be accused in the papers of having "run down" a 747 on final?

Having instruments in good working condition in an airplane at night is a lot better than not having them. But they are not absolute assurance against getting lost. And once lost, getting reoriented in the dark is a lot more complicated than it is in the daytime. Don't scoot around the sky willy-nilly, hoping to pick up some sort of useful signal. Call somebody. That's what the com radio is for, and those characters on the ground don't have a lot to do at night, so don't be embarrassed to tell them your predicament and ask them to help. There are a variety of means by which ground personnel can get you back on course. They can give you a DF steer, they can pick you up on radar and give you vectors back to the course you thought you were on, or they can even give you a surveillance radar approach to within a mile on an airport.

Once, on my way from Midland, Texas, to El Paso, I must have been daydreaming, or rather, nightdreaming, because suddenly I realized that I wasn't receiving a damn thing on my VOR receiver, and I didn't have ADF then. I was sure I was on the right course so I just kept on flying until things got a bit nervous. Well, to make a long and palm-sweating story short, I must have had a quartering tailwind I didn't know about because I had happily flown right into Mexico, and it took a bit of doing to eventually get me turned around and on course to El Paso. That was one time when I could have saved myself a lot of nerves and fuel if I had had the brains to contact someone on radio, instead of stubbornly trying to find my way all by my lonesome. Remember, when you don't seem to be able to reach an FSS or tower, look up the frequency for the Center Sector in which you believe yourself to be and call them. They can nearly always be reached and, unless you're very low, more probably than not they can find you on radar. These frequencies are printed on the Jeppesens and in the bottom margin of the Sectionals.

If you're in trouble and your radios aren't doing their thing but you have a working transponder, tune it for about a minute or so to 7700 and then to 7600. The 7700 will alert the controller that there is an aircraft in trouble, and the switch to 7600 means that the trouble is the radio. He will then try to contact you on 121.5 and, if that doesn't work, on any of the VOR frequencies which, based on your location, you ought to be able to receive. Chances are, you'll receive on one of those frequencies and he can then talk to you and have you reply by using the ident button on the transponder.

One more thought. Since the speaker and microphone are not only the cheapest parts of your radio system, but also the ones most likely to give trouble, spend a few dollars and buy a spare microphone and headset. Then, if you find you can't transmit or receive or both, plug in the spare and chances are better than 50:50 that you'll be back in business.

Also, if there is more than one navigation radio in the airplane, use not just one. Use them all, all the time. Check their readings against one another. In that way you'll find out immediately if something is going awry with one or the other. In addition, it gives you something to do and keeps you from falling asleep.

Chapter 10
Seeing in the Dark

Though it may seem a trifle incongruous, considering how little there is to see at night, night vision is important to night flying. And we are talking here about several kinds of night vision, night vision inside the cockpit and night vision outside the cockpit.

Inside the cockpit the pilot must be able to read his instruments by whatever light is available. And he must be able to read his charts.

Outside the cockpit he must be able to see and recognize the meaning of lights on the ground, be they nearby or in the distance. And he must be able to distinguish between dozens of shades of dark-grey-black which represent topographical features, clouds, haze, smoke, fog, and other meteorological phenomena.

Let's start inside the cockpit.

THE INSTRUMENTS

In some airplanes the instruments are equipped with integral rim lighting or with post lights, the intensity of which can be adjusted and which make instrument reading easy. Others simply have a kind of adjustable red floodlight which usually leaves part of the panel in shadow or darkness. It too can usually be dimmed or turned up bright.

While en route in clear weather, many pilots prefer to keep the cockpit lights fairly bright, since it makes monitoring the instruments easier and less tiring, and there is really nothing much to be gained by looking at the darkness outside. There is nothing much wrong with that (the strobes or rotating beacons of other aircraft are easy to see at night, even with the instrument lights all the way up), but one should reduce cockpit illumination to a minimum at least 15 or 20 minutes before reaching a point of landing, in order to give the eyes a chance to get adjusted to the darkness and thus improve the ability to see outside the cockpit during approach and landing.

Also, if the weather is kind of iffy, one might find that it is preferable to fly with the cockpit lights on low (and occasionally turned off altogether) in order to keep abreast of what is going on outside the airplane.

THE CHARTS

Reading charts in the cockpit at night can get to be a real chore. If the pilot has good eyesight and the red cockpit light is turned up high, he may be able to read the Jeppesens, as they are printed in blue and green, both of which colors appear as shades of dark grey or black under red light. But reading the Sectionals or WACs in red light is considerably more difficult as much of the information is represented in colors which contain red, and are thus either reduced or completely washed out by the red light.

The alternative is to either turn on the dome light or to use a flashlight. The dome light, assuming it is of sufficient brightness, is easier to use because it leaves both hands free. A flashlight must be held in one hand while the pilot fights with the chart with the other.

If there are clouds around, they are easier to see with the cockpit lights turned down low.

There are sort of gooseneck flashlights which one can stick in one's breast pocket, but they always seem to be pointing in the wrong direction. Some airplanes are equipped with so-called map lights, but most of those are good only when one knows the particular portion of a chart one wants to study. If a large part of a Sectional or WAC must be examined, they just don't illuminate a large enough area.

One way or the other, regardless of the quality of the lighting built into the airplane, no one should ever attempt to fly at night without a flashlight with good, fresh batteries. It's absolutely essential during preflight, repeatedly while in flight, and after landing to simplify tying down the airplane.

Pilots who, like myself, find the under normal light conditions they can do fine without eyeglasses, but who do need them to read things like the phonebook when no bright direct light is available, should always remember to take their glasses along. All that stuff printed on the charts is just too small to be read easily in the kind of light available in airplanes.

Using our eyes to see outside the cockpit at night requires a bit of practice. The reason is that when there is little light, we use different portions of the eye than we do under conditions of bright light.

The portion of the eye which accepts whatever the eye looks at and then transmits that image via the optic nerve to the brain, consists of two types of receivers, the rods and the cones. The cones are positioned in the central area of the retina and are tapered nerve ends. They function best when there is ample light. In addition they have the capability of distinguishing colors. Surrounding this area are cylindrical rods. They are largely responsible for our peripheral vision. They are color blind, but have the capability of becoming increasingly sensitive under low light conditions and are thus our primary means of seeing at night. It takes about 30 to 40 minutes for the rods to become fully sensitized and even a brief flash of white light will desensitize them and the process has to start all over again. They are not affected by red light which is why most cockpit illumination is red.

But, since the rods are not able to receive an image input from straight in front, the eye, during conditions of very little light, has, in fact, a blind spot right in the center. Thus, in order to effectively use the rods to see, we should use our eyes by slowly sweeping the area to be seen, radar fashion. In this manner our peripheral vision will pick up the images which prove to be invisible when we stare at them straight ahead.

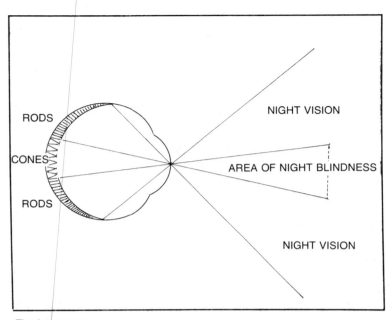

The human eye.

A brightly moonlit night usually provides enough light to permit the cones to funciton, while anything less than that can only be seen with the rods.

At times when good night vision is important, but we find that we do have to use some light to look at a chart or something, such as during the last 15 or 20 minutes prior to landing when we want to look up a tower frequency, for instance, it is good practice to keep one eye tightly closed, and read the chart with only the other eye. That way we can retain the visual acuity in one eye.

Night tends to produce some visual illusions and pilots ought to be aware of them and to be able to recognize them for what they are. One such is caused when we stare at a stationary light for any length of time. After a while it will begin to seem to move. This is called autokinetic effect, and its cause is not clearly understood. To avoid this illusion, it is best to intermittently look away from the light. When looking back at it it will have returned to its original and true position, only to start wandering again after a few moments of staring at it.

Another disconcerting illusion is the sudden disappearance of something you thought you had seen, like the rotating beacon of an airport in the distance. You see it for a moment, then, trying to determine its exact location, it's suddenly gone. The reason is, of course, the blind spot which we talked about before. We saw the rotating beacon with our rods. This caused us to look directly at the point at which we thought we saw it, and thus we are putting it into the blind center portion of the eye and it simply vanishes.

Ideally, one should look about 10 degrees to one side or the other of an object to be seen in the near-dark. That permits the rods to pick it up and to paint it on the retina which, in turn, transmits it to the optic nerve to be forwarded to the brain.

This sort of looking off to one side or the other of something we really want to see is a lot easier to talk about than to do. Especially when what we are searching for are any of those slight variations in the shadings of darkness which are indicative of clouds or unlighted terrain features. It can be pure hell trying to figure out the significance of a slightly lighter or darker area. Is it something to be avoided or just a bit of haze or smoke picking up a minute amount of light or causing an equally minute degree of shadow?

There is simply no way of saying with any degree of certainty that such and such a visual impression is the result of such and such a specific phenomenon. Only long hours spent in cockpits at night will gain the pilot the experience to recognize such shapes for what they are, and even then he is likely to make the wrong decision occasionally.

As an example, I remember seeing an area of somewhat greater darkness above a slightly lighter area in the distance ahead. I decided that the darker area was clear sky while the lighter portion seemed like some thin cloud or haze. Knowing my destination (El Paso) to be clear, I began to climb to be able to get over whatever it was I was looking at. Well, I climbed for quite a while before I realized that the darker area was actually a cloud while the lighter area turned out to be the one I should have been heading for in the first place. Then, at other times, the exact opposite proved to be the case.

The ability of the eye to do a good job for us is largely dependent on an adequate supply of oxygen in the body and a diet which provides the required quantity of vitamin A. The oxygen supply is affected by the altitude at which we fly, and by the amount of smoking we do prior to takeoff and during the flight. Altitude is something we can't (and don't want to) get away from. We should simply realize that when flying at 10,000 or 12,000 feet without supplementary oxygen, our ability to see at night is going to be impaired to some degree. Smoking, on the other hand, is something we can do something about. Ideally, we should not smoke for several hours before a night flight, and not during it. Admittedly to some of us—this writer included—not smoking for several hours is close to impossible. So, if we can't stop altogether, let's at least cut it down to a bare minimum. Chewing on an unlit cigarette helps quite a bit, as does eating candy or peanuts or something.

As far as vitamin A is concerned, it is contained in ample quantity in most fresh vegetables (especially carrrots), fruits, eggs and other common foods. Taking huge doses of vitamin A as a supplement has no noticeable beneficial effect, unless our eating habits are such that our food supplies an insufficient amount (which is fairly unlikely).

By being forced to try and see when there is really nothing much to look at, our eyes can get tired. Normally, after undergoing unusual eye strain, we would rest the eyes by closing them for a while. The temptation to do this while flying at night is considerable. But it does present a very real danger. The danger is that we might just fall asleep, and while the airplane itself couldn't care less whether the pilot is awake or asleep, it is obviously not a brilliant idea to leave it to its own devices for any length of time, as it might just run out of fuel in the tank being used or fly into a mountain, neither of which is a healthy way to conclude a night flight.

Chapter 11
Pilot Reports

In daytime flying we usually have easy access to a plethora of information about weather and flight conditions. There are the hourly sequence reports broadcast by most FSSs over the VOR frequencies at 15 minutes past each hour. We can listen to other aircraft asking for and receiving all manner of information which may or may not be applicable to our own flight. We can listen to other pilots making PIREPs. Or we can contact any FSS within range and ask for whatever information we feel we need in order to make intelligent decisions.

At night much of this stream of information tends to dry up. For reasons for which I have yet to find an intelligent explanation, most FSSs stop making their hourly reports after dark. The flying activity is reduced to a minimum, so there are few conversations to listen to. And, with few pilots actually in the air, there are less PIREPs being made. What is left is our ability to contact the guys at the FSSs and ask for information.

When we do this we'll often find, especially during the hours between midnight and dawn, that those fellows are delighted to have someone to talk to, and that they tend to be many times as helpful as they are in the daytime with its increased workload.

On the other hand, night is the time when our ability to see ahead and judge conditions by visual means is reduced to next to nil, and we desperately need to be aware of possible changes in the weather conditions ahead. All of us who spend much time in the red-tinted gloom of a night cockpit could do each other a valuable service if we would make it a habit to report even slightly unusual conditions which could be of interest to others. In addition we should ask for PIREPs and ask the FSS specialists to solicit PIREPs as an encouragement to others. The trouble is that we frequently have the feeling that after reporting something, the report just sort of languishes at the FSS and never gets anywhere and, as a result, we may feel that it's all a waste of time.

In my own experience I can recall many instances when, say, approaching what looked like an overcast more or less at the level at which I was flying, I would call an FSS and ask if any reports on the tops were available. While the direct answer as often as not might have been negative, in many instances some other pilot would get on the line and say that he was currently flying along the route indicated by me, and the tops were at a level which made the decision to climb to a higher altitude and continue VFR on top seem logical.

On the other hand, the opposite might be true. A pilot may call and say that he is in solid IFR conditions which would then cause me to either drop down lower or consider filing IFR myself.

Safe night flying depends to a greater degree on constant awareness of changes in weather and flight conditions, and pilot reports, representing real-time information gathered on the spot, are one of the most valuable means of obtaining the needed information.

Chapter 12

Using RNAV at Night

The immediate reaction to the idea of using RNAV (area navigation) at night would seem to contradict all that has been said about flying doglegs instead of a straight line in order to always be within a reasonable distance of a lighted airport. But the fact is that RNAV can be of great value if it is used correctly.

For those who are not thoroughly familiar with the way in which RNAV works, let's first examine the principles on which its operation is based in some detail.

The kind of RNAV were are talking about here (there are other kinds, inertial navigation and VLF/Omega, which are not applicable to our subject) consists of three basic ingredients: The standard VOR receiver, a DME and a course-line computer (CLC). With these three instruments in the cockpit, we can electronically move existing VORs from their actual location to any other spot on the ground within a reasonable distance, usually 50 or 60 miles.

The way it works is like this: We dial into the CLC the radial from a particular VORTAC on which the selected location is, and we measure the distance from the VORTAC on the chart and dial that in too. The CLC uses that information and computes the appropriate coordinates and electronically creates a waypoint which is the common phrase used for such an imaginary VOR location.

Instead of pointing to the actual VORTAC, the OBI now directs us to the waypoint and the DME tells us how far we are from it.

In normal use, RNAV permits the pilot to create a ruler-straight route from Point A to Point B without regard of airways or

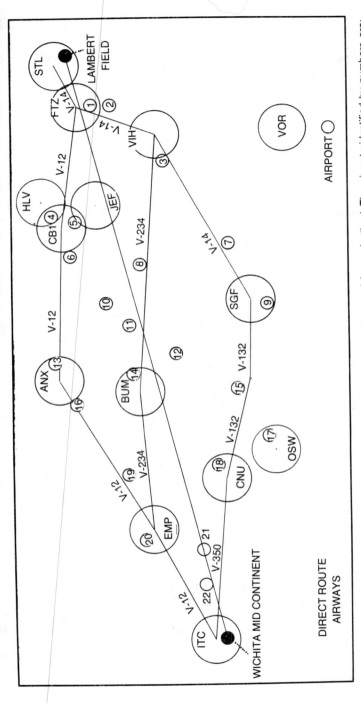

St. Louis to Wichita. (This chart is considerably simplified and should not be used for navigation.) The airports identified by numbers are:
1—Washington, MO; 2—St. Clair; 3—Rolla; 4—Wood Memorial; 5—Columbia Regional; 6—Viertel; 7—Lebanon; 8—Wulff Harbor; 9—Springfield; 10—Sedalia; 11—Clinton Memorial; 12—Nevada; 13—East Kansas City; 14—Butler; 15—Lamar; 16—Johnson County; 17—Oswego; 18—Chanute; 19—Ottawa; 20—Emporia; 21—Eureka; 22—El Dorado.

DIRECT ROUTE
AIRWAYS

AIRPORT ◯

71

the location of ground-based navigation aids. It thus results in shorter trip times and, in turn, in fuel savings. (It can also be used to fly published RNAV approaches and is useful as an aid in flying all manner of non-precision approaches, but these applications have nothing to do with its usefulness in relation to night flight.)

Its usefulness at night is its ability to constantly pinpoint a usable airport with an uncanny degree of accuracy, and accuracy which can become vitally important in the event that some sort of engine malfunction or other emergency makes it necessary for us to get on the ground in a hurry.

Let's design an imaginary flight and see how it works in practice.

We want to go from Lambert Field in St. Louis to Wichita. The fact we can determine immediately by looking at the charts is that there is no direct Victory Airway along anything resembling a straight line between those two points. The accompanying simplified chart depicts the direct course between the two points, the appropriate airways, the location of VORs and of airports equipped with rotating beacons.

The difference in distance when flying either the direct route or using the airways is, in fact, less significant than it would appear to be from looking at the chart:

Flying a straight line, the distance is 340 nm. Going from Lambert direct to FTZ and then taking V-12 via CBI, ANX, EMP to ITC adds up to 357 nm. Or, going direct from Lambert Field to FTZ and then using V-14 via VIH to SGF and then V-132 to CNU and V-350 to ITC totals 366 nm. The third possibility, Lambert direct to FTZ, then V-14 to VIH, then V-234 via BUM to EMP and then V-12 to ITC amounts to 358 nm.

Converted to flight times, assuming a 140-knot cruise and no wind, this figures out to two hours and 25 minutes for the direct route; two hours and 33 minutes for Victor-12; two hours and 37 minutes for the southern route via Springfield; and two hours and 33.5 minutes for the route via Vichy, Butler and Emporia.

Assuming now that we plan to fly at 8,500 feet msl and figuring the average terrain elevation in the area at roughly 1,000 feet, we would, in the event of an engine malfunction, have to glide down some 7,500 feet. Let's say the average glide will produce a descent rate of 500 fpm at a forward speed of 120 knots. Based on these assumptions, we would have an opportunity to reach any point within 30 nm of the point at which the engine malfunction occurred.

If we now draw a 30-nm circle around each of the tighted airports, we will find that there are only very few moments during

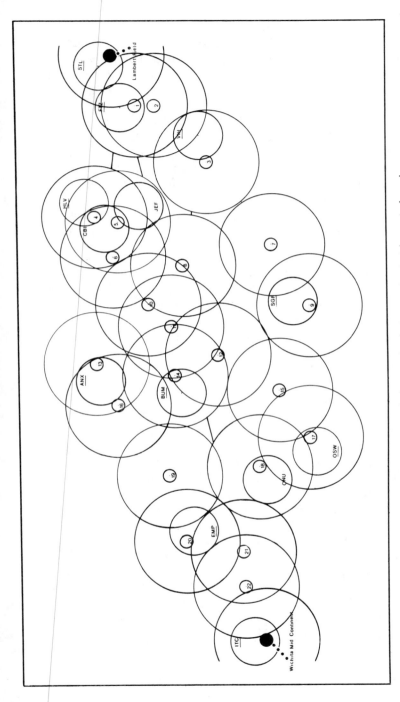

If we draw of 30-nm circle around each of the lighted airports, there are only a few on-route stretches out of reach.

73

which no such airport could be reached, regardless of the route chosen. We have marked those danger areas on the chart and find that on the direct route there are a 2.5-nm and a 15-nm stretch beyond gliding distance of an airport, while on V-12 there is a 10-mile stretch and on V-14 and V-234 just tiny one or two-mile blind spots.

On the other hand, it would be rather foolish to assume that that 30-nm gliding distance is a realistic one. It is affected by all sorts of considerations. One is the speed with which the pilot recognizes the emergency and takes appropriate action. Another might be the time it takes to decide which airport to head for. Another has to do with the prevailing winds. We have assumed no wind, but we also know that, for all practical purposes, there is no such thing. A headwind will reduce the distance covered in the glide, while a tailwind will increase it. And lastly, we can't very well assume that we will be able to end our glide in an uninterrupted straight-in approach and landing. We may have to circle to get to the right runway, there may be conflicting traffic (even though, an aircraft having declared an emergency, has the right of way over any other aircraft, except a balloon.)

With this in mind it would be a lot more sensible to consider our actual glide potential as, say 15 nm, which changes the picture somewhat. Suddenly there are big holes both, on the airways and on the direct course and it would seem that the prudent pilot might do better to pick a route which will, if not eliminate, then at least minimize these stretches from which a safe emergency landing must be considered doubtful at best.

What would seem to emerge as the safest route is somewhat modified zigzag going from Lambert Field direct to the Foristell VOR (FTZ), from there along the 270-degree radial from FTZ to the intersection of the 231-degree radial from the Hallsville VOR (HLV) and the 302-degree radial from the Jefferson City VOR (JEF). Then turn left and fly along the 231-degree radial from HLV for a distance of 120 nm to the intersection of the 110-degree radial from Chanute VOR (CNU) and the 040-degree radial from Oswego VOR (OSW). Then turn right to a heading of 275 degrees and continue for 65 nm to the intersection of the 200-degree radial from the Emporia VOR (EMP) and the 084-degree radial from the Wichita VOR (ITC). Then make a slight course correction to the left and fly a 261-degree heading direct to Wichita MidContinent Airport.

Going this way the total distance is 382 nm, somewhat longer than any of the airways and 42 nm longer than the direct route, a difference of 18 minutes.

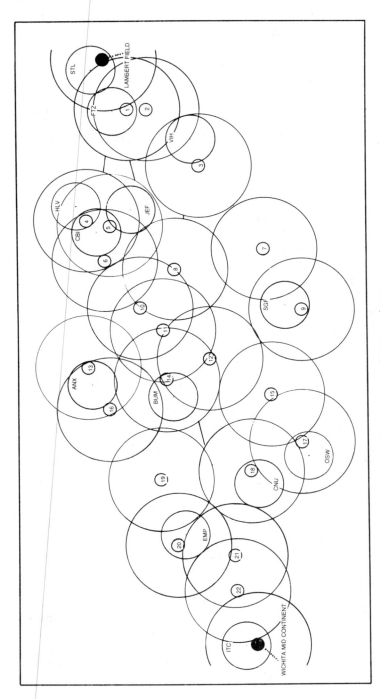

Suddenly there are long stretches during which we will be unable to glide to an airport.

On the other hand, if we add up to total distances during which we are beyond the 15-nm gliding distance of a lighted airport the comparison looks like this:

STL to ITC direct: 167 nm out of a total distance of 340 nm, or 49.1 percent of the time.

STL direct FTZ then V-12 to ITC: 128 nm out of a total of 357 nm, or 35.9 percent of the time.

STL direct FTZ then V-14, V-132, V350 to ITC; 140 nm out of a total distance of 366 nm, or 38.3 percent of the time.

STL direct FTZ then V-14, V-234, V-12 to ITC: 139 nm out of a total distance of 358 nm, or 38.8 percent of the total time.

The suggested route: 89 nm out of a total distance of 382 nm, or 23.3 percent of the time.

All right, so it does look as if it would be considerably safer to fly the slightly longer dogleg. So not let's look at different ways in which this can best be accomplished, with and without RNAV capability in the airplane.

FLIGHT A

Conditions: The weather report for the entire Missouri and Kansas areas calls for generally clear skies, visibilities 10 miles or better, with only occasional high cirrus. The winds are forecast to be light and variable at 3,000 and 6,000, 10 knots from 300 degrees at 9,000 and 15 knots from 280 degrees at 12,000.

The airplane: A Bellanca Super Viking equipped with conventional dual navcom, ADF and an Edo-Aire/Mitchell Century I autopilot. No DME or RNAV. Average cruising speed at 55 percent of power is 141 knots. The range with full tanks is somewhat in excess of 700 nm with the kind of reserves considered adequate for night flight.

Miscellaneous: The pilot, private ticket, SEL and MEL, 1,800 hours, 120 hours at night, not instrument rated; he will be flying alone. It is a day in early September, and he plans to take off at 8:30 p.m. Central Daylight Time and expects to arrive at Wichita around 11:30 p.m. CDT. There will be a quarter moon, but moonrise is not until 10:45 p.m., so it won't do him much good.

Takeoff: It is 8:28 p.m. when he calls Ground Control at Lambert and is cleared to Runway 30R and is given the Departure Control frequency with which he must remain in contact while within the limits of the St. Louis TCA. He tunes his com-2 radio to that frequency, taxies out and when ready switches the com-1 from Ground to Tower, saying that he is ready to go.

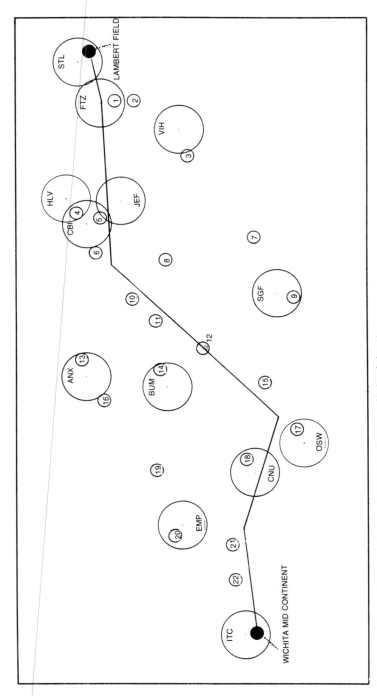

The longer route keeps us more safely within gliding distance of lighted airports.

Cleared for takeoff he takes off, contacts Departure and, upon his request, is cleared direct to the Foristell VOR. His nav-1 receiver, tuned to FTZ (110.8 MHz), picks up the VOR signal shortly after lift-off and he turns left and keeps the needle centered while climbing to 8,500 feet, the altitude he has decided to fly.

Once clear of the TCA he bids Departure good night and roughly 15 minutes after lift-off he crosses to FTZ VOR. He now tunes the OBS to the 270-degree radial from FTZ and flies outbound on this radial, tuning his nav-2 receiver to the Jefferson City VOR (JEF, 110.2 MHz). He knows from studying the chart prior to takeoff that he'll want to hold this course for 80 nm at which point he'll be turning southwesterly in order to fly the selected route which will keep him within a reasonably safe distance of a lighted airport most of the time.

Now level at 8,500 feet he is guessing his ground speed to be about 135 knots, based on the forecast wind at that altitude. At that speed it should take him 36 minutes to cover those 80 nm and, remembering having crossed FTZ at 8:46, he moves the red indicator on his clock to 22 minutes past the hour.

Somewhere, about 20 or so minutes after crossing FTZ, the signal from that station begins to fade and the OFF flag keeps popping up on the nav-1. He now tunes it to the Hallsville VOR (HLV, 114.2 MHz), tuning the OBS to the 231-degree radial.

With the nav-1 now tuned to HLV/231 and the nav-2 to JEF/302, he no longer has any direct guidance from his nav receivers and is depending on the autopilot to hold the 270-degree course. He has, of course, been aware that he has had to hold a five-degree heading correction to the right to allow for the quartering headwind. In other words, he continues holding a 275-degree heading under the assumption that he'll arrive reasonably close to the intersection of the two radials he has tuned into his nav receivers.

Right now the needles in both OBIs are pegged, the nav-1 to the right and the nav-2 to the left. Noting on his Sectional that there are two standard broadcast stations more or less straight ahead, he turns on his ADF. KWRT at Boonville is closest to the correct direction, but it is marked "Days Only" but figuring that as far as radio stations are concerned, 9 p.m. might still be considered day, he tunes the ADF to its frequency of 1370 and is rewarded with a needle movement fluctuating back and forth between straight ahead, some 10 or 15 degrees to the right and some five degrees to the left of the nose. Knowing ADF indications at night to be relatively unreliable, he figures that that is good enough and he continues on.

The weather report calls for generally clear skies with occasional high cirrus.

This is the longest stretch of the entire flight during which he will be beyond gliding distance of a usable airport, a fact which is verified by the absence of any green-and-white rotating beacons among the relatively sparse amount of lights below, though far off to the right he does occasionally see the more or less uninterrupted line of headlights from the cars traveling east or west on I-70.

After another five or six minutes he becomes aware of a rotating beacon ahead and slightly to the right of his nose, and he assumes that if he is where be believes himself to be that this must be Columbia Regional Airport (#5 on our simplified chart). He plays with the knob on the nav-2 OBS and finds that the needle centers at 030 degrees which, he guesses, puts him about 12 or so nm southeast of Columbia Regional.

He resets the nav-1 OBS and flies on, paying little attention to the ADF, though its needle is beginning to settle down somewhat, pointing primarily just a few degrees to the right of the nose. At 9:18 p.m. the nav-2 needle begins to jiggle and to slowly move off the peg and toward the middle, while the nav-1 needle remains pegged at the left. This would seem to indicate that he is slightly to the right of his course and he makes a 10-degree course correction to the left.

Soon the nav-1 needle moves too and it is about half way between the peg and the center when the nav-2 needle centers, meaning that it is time to make his turn to a 231-degree heading which he does instantly and moments later the centering of the nav-1 needle tells him that he is now crossing the point he had been aiming for. The time is 9:23 p.m., one minute later than his original estimate. Not bad.

Now established on the 231-degree radial from HLV he finds that he has to hold a seven-degree correction to the right which seems to indicate to him that the wind is somewhat stronger than had been forecast and more westerly and less northerly.

For the time being the autopilot is coupled to the HLV VOR and automatically correct for the wind drift. But this leg is 130 nm long and he knows that after a while he will lose the HLV signal and will have to continue on course as best as he can.

Based on his estimate of the effect of the wind on his ground speed, he figures it will take him just about one hour to fly that 130-nm distance, and he leaves the red indicator on his clock at 22 minutes past the hour. All the while he keeps paying reasonably close attention to the rotating beacons on the airports along his route which appear one after another on is right.

Meanwhile it hasn't taken long until he lost the HLV signal, but figuring that he can use the Columbia VOR for maybe another 10 minutes or so, he switches the nav-1 over to its frequency (CBI, 111.2 MHz) and finds that by making just the tiniest correction with the OBS, he can let the autopilot keep him on his course.

The lights of the Sedalia Airport (#10 on the chart) have passed at his right and those of the Clinton Memorial Airport (#11 on the chart) are coming into view to the right of the nose when the signal from CBI starts to fade and he uncouples the autopilot, letting it hold its heading as best as it can without input from a VOR.

The next airport is supposed to be directly on his route. It is Nevada and there is a broadcast station, KNEM, frequency 1240. He tunes the ADF to it and the ADF needle again does its dance but eventually does settle more or less on the nose.

Just to keep himself busy he tunes in the Butler VOR (BUM, 115.9 MHz) and, by playing with the OBS, watches his progress southwestward.

At about five minutes of 10 p.m. the lights of Nevada Airport appear right straight ahead and at exactly 10:01 p.m. he overflies the airport. This is a few minutes later than it should have been, indicating that there is more headwind component than he had anticipated, but certainly not enough to worry about.

The distance from the Nevada Airport to where he is planning to make his right turn is 44 nm which he figures should take him about 20 minutes. He tunes in the two VORs which he will need to

He keep the needle centered while climbing to 8,500 feet.

identify the point, even though he knows that he is still beyond reliable reception distance. Nav-1 is tuned to Oswego (OSW, 117.6 MHz) and nav-2 is tuned to Chanute (CNU, 109.2), and within less than five minutes both do start to come in. The intersection he is looking for is the crossing point of the 110-degree radial from CNU and the 040-degree radial from OSW and he adjusts the OBSs in both navs to the appropriate radials.

With one minor last-minute course correction he does reach the intersection of those radials at 20 minutes past 10 p.m., actually two minutes ahead of his previous estimate. He now turns right to a heading of 275 degrees and tunes one of the nav receivers to Wichita (ITC, 113.8 MHz) which, though still out of reach, he knows will have to come in reasonably soon. He is now about 120 nm from his destination and expects that he'll be on the ground in Wichita not later than 11:20 p.m.

Though in his pre-flight planning he had carefully figured out another intersection of two VOR radials at which to make a slight course correction to the left to take him straight to the Wichita Airport, once he does pick up the ITC VOR he decides, the hell with it and flies straight to it, contacting Wichita Tower as soon as the lights of the airport come into view to the left of his nose.

His wheels touch ground at 11:16 p.m. and he taxies in. End of flight.

FLIGHT B

Everything is the same as with the previously described flight, except that the aircraft is equipped with DME and RNAV, and the pilot has prepared a list of waypoints to use in order to accomplish the selected route. These waypoints are spaced more or less equidistant to permit him to always fly directly to such a waypoint. See accompanying illustration.

The list of these waypoints, prepared prior to takeoff, looks like this:

HLV/114.2/140/31
HLV/114.2/231/45
BUM/115.9/075/43
BUM/115.9/171/34
OSW/117.6/040/20
OSW/117.6/315/27
EMP/112.8/200/34

Since the RNAV in his airplane is one of the less expensive types which permit him to dial in only one waypoint at a time (some RNAVs will accept large numbers of waypoints in advance in consecutive order), he will have only the first one entered into the CLC before takeoff, using the other nav receiver in the conventional manner.

Thus, after takeoff, he flies to FTZ direct and then departs FTZ on the 270-degree radial. At first the HLV VOR will be too far away to be usable, but as he continues on the course, it comes in some time before reaching the waypoint and starts to display the waypoint in the other OBI. He can now fly to it simply by keeping the needle centered.

Once having reached the waypoint, he enters the new coordinates into the CLC and immediately waypoint number two appears and he can continue flying the course by reference to the needle.

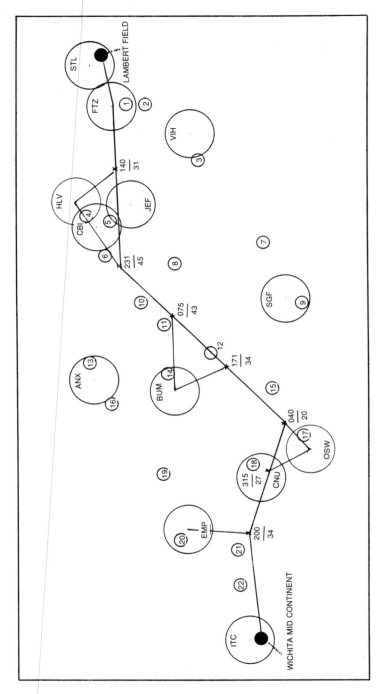

The pilot has placed waypoints more or less equidistant along his route.

Having passed the second waypoint and made the left turn to 231 degrees he can fly this radial outbound for as long as his receivers are able to pick up the signal from HLV. He cannot use the JEF or CBI VORs because, not being VORTACs, they are unusable for DME and, in turn, for RNAV.

By the time the signal from HLV begins to fade he tunes in BUM and enters the coordinates for the next waypoint into the CLC. He should, by now, be within reception distance from BUM and waypoint number three will appear, as will number four, after he changes the coordinates accordingly.

After passing it he can continue outbound from the waypoint until reaching reception distance from OSW, at which point he dials in number five. (He cannot use the CNU VOR for this purpose because, again, it is not a VORTAC.)

Continuing in this manner all the way to Wichita, he will have flown the entire route with considerable precision, despite the fact that there was only one VOR actually on the route which he had decided to fly. Throughout all this he will have, of course, kept track of the location in the various airports along the route, just in case.

RNAV, more than any other cockpit instrument, permits the pilot to use his own preference when planning and then flying a particular mission. For instance, instead of using his RNAV as described above, the pilot might have put all of his waypoints right over actual lighted airports and thus could have flown from one usable airport to the next, always knowing that, if an emergency should arise, there would be an airport straight ahead at the exact distance displayed by his DME.

Conversely, he might decide to fly the Victor Airways in a conventional manner, using one nav receiver for navigation. He can then use the second nav receiver in conjunction with his RNAV equipment to tell him where the various airports are, and, though in this instance he whould not be actually flying to the waypoints, the waypoints would simply be there for him to know which way to turn if a sudden landing became imperative. And, in addition to knowing which way to turn, his DME would also tell him how far he would have to glide in order to get there.

RNAV is not cheap. The DME and CLC together will cost anywhere from $5,000 on up, and if its only usefulness would be to make flying at night safer, it would probably not be worth its cost (unless, of course, it one day saved your life, in which case only you can know how much it was really worth to you). But once a pilot gets experiences in using RNAV, day or night, IFR or VFR, he will suddenly realize that this little electronic marvel is such a fanstastic instrument that he'll wonder how he ever got along without it.

Chapter 13
Those Long Winter Nights

Winter flying brings a variety of problems which don't exist during the rest of the year, but, strangely, in some respects night flying in the dead of winter is often easier than at other times. Still, special precautions must be taken, and it is only natural that, in view of the preponderance of hours of darkness during those months, the need to fly after dark increases.

Basically, of course, the principles are the same. You will want to fly high, and you will want to plan the route of flight to stay within a reasonable distance of lighted airports for as much of the time as is possible. But winter means snow in many parts of the country and a considerable percentage of otherwise perfectly good airports is sadly deficient in snow-removal capabilities. And even when such snow-removal equipment is available, it is not likely to be put to use if there has been an evening snow fall, until the next morning at the earliest.

With this in mind, flight planning becomes a much more important exercise.

Let's say we want to fly from Phoenix to Minneapolis, leaving Phoenix at around five p.m. The distance is just under 1,100 nm and the flight will therefore require a fuel stop somewhere along the way. The straightest and, in turn, shortest possible route would pass just south of Farmington, New Mexico, go right over Colorado Springs and North Platte, Nebraska, pass south of Sioux Falls and from there straight into Minneapolis. Let's just assume it's late January, meaning that while the temperature in Phoenix may be pleasantly in the 70s or 80s, most of the rest of the country, especially the northern half, has been suffering through a series of storms which, intermittently, have dumped considerable amounts of snow on the ground.

In addition, winter weather is much less predictable. Those slow-moving warm fronts which tend to inhibit the VFR pilot during the summer are absent now. Instead there are smaller, more violent and faster moving fronts which slide down from Canada, Alaska and the northern Pacific, spread across much of the Rocky Mountain area, then move eastward into the Middle West and eventually turn northeasterly to leave their imprint on New England before disappearing out over the Atlantic.

Along our proposed route we are likely to find the ground below covered with snow after having flown about 200 nm northeastward and from then on for much of the rest of the way. With Colorado Springs being just short of half way (just under 500 nm from PHX) it would probably be the ideal fuel stop. In addition it is a major airport and can be expected to keep its runways clear of snow or ice.

Now let's examine this route. Admittedly, it is likely to present a greater number of problems than can be expected to be encountered on most flights, but for that very reason it seems an ideal example.

Phoenix Sky Harbor is at an elevation of 1,128 feet. We'll be taking off just around sunset or a little after, but there is likely to be a reasonable amount of glow left in the sky to permit seeing ground features for another half hour or so. We'll be flying over sparsely populated, extremely inhospitable country with few places where an emergency landing could be made successfully even during daylight, so we better be sure that the airplane we are flying is in tiptop condition.

After lift-off we would be heading northeast at 030 degrees and within about 80 nm we'll be crossing the Mogollon Mesa which rises to just under 8,000 feet and it would be prudent for us to be at a 9,500 foot altitude at the very least.

By now it will be dark with only occasional specks of light to be seen on the ground. We would continue on course, aware that we'll be passing about 20 nm to the right of the lighted airport at Winslow, Arizona, and flying right over Holbrook, Arizona, which also has a lighted airport. In this area the ground below us averages about 5,000 feet with no major mountains to worry about until we get near the border of Arizona and New Mexico. There we'll be crossing the Defiance Plateau which rises to around 8,000 feet and a few miles farther on the Chuska Mountains at their southern edge. Consider-

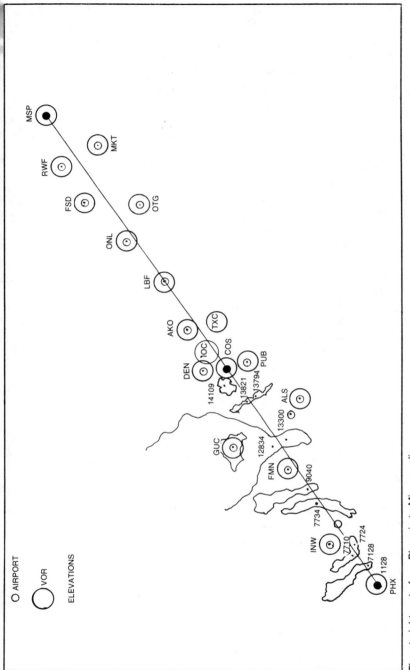

The straight route from Phoenix to Minneapolis.

ing the time of the year, these mountains, which slightly north of our course rise to around 9,500 feet, can be expected to be snow covered. This is where the advantage of winter comes in. If there is any kind of a moon, these snow-covered rocks can be clearly seen, and even if there is no moon, the light from the stars is usually enough to permit us to see the ground. (If it is overcast we shouldn't be flying around here at night. Those clouds have a proclivity for obscuring mountaintops and it would be sheer folly to try and negotiate the Rockies VFR on a cloudy night, no matter what time of the year it is.)

By now we should be able to see the lights of Farmington, New Mexico, and the rotating beacon of its airport which will slide by below, some 15 nm to our left. It should be remembered that the visibilities in this high country tend to be 50 miles or better, thus lighted airports or the lights of towns can be seen for great distances. Pilots not accustomed to flying here tend to underestimate the distance to a particular landmark simply because it can be seen so clearly.

When we get near Farmington, we better start climbing to a higher altitude. The mountains ahead are the southern portion of the San Juans, and there are peaks all over the place rising to 12,000 and 13,000 feet. How high we actually climb depends on the amount of light available. The mountains will be completely snow-covered (they are about nine months out of the year) and if there is a halfway decent moon out, we can probably stay safely away from the higher peaks and get through at, say, 11,500 or so. (We don't have to worry about keeping to the cardinal altitudes, as they are effective only above 3,000 agl, and we're bound to be a lot closer to the ground than that.)

Once atop those mountains we'll be able to see the lights of two lighted airports in the distance to the right of our nose. Those are Alamosa and San Luis Valley, both in southern Colorado. We'll be passing to the left of both those airports, with the ground below us having dropped down to about 7,600 feet or so.

The next ridge to cross is the northern end of the Sangre de Cristo mountain range and we should be passing between two peaks, one 13,621 feet high, and the other 13,794. In order to safely do this we may briefly have to get up to over 12,000 feet, but it's a narrow range and we shouldn't have to be up there for more than five or ten minutes.

From here on it's all downhill. We'll be spotting the lights of Fremont County Airport at Canon City, Colorado, just about straight ahead, and once there, the lights of Colorado Springs will

We'll be flying over inhospitable country with few places where an emergency landing could be made successfully.

outline the southern slope of Pikes Peak which lies just to the left of our course. (There is a small restricted area just south of Pikes Peak with a road running along its edge. As long as we keep barely to the left of that road, we'll know that we are remaining clear of that area.)

Peterson Field at Colorado Springs is at an elevation of 6,172, so the better part of valor would be to stay reasonably high until we know that we've got the airport made.

Depending on the kind of airplane we've been flying, it should now be about 8:20 or nine p.m. and it would probably be a good idea to have a cup of coffee and a bite to eat while the airplane is being fueled.

Feeling refreshed and wide awake, we'll be back in the air by about 9:30 or 10 p.m., prepared for the rest of the flight which, though somewhat duller, will at least lead us gradually into more and more densely populated areas. In all probability there will be snow on the ground all the rest of the way, dissected by the dark lines representing roads, highways, and railroads.

But those more densely populated areas are not exactly right around the corner. After lift-off from Colorado Springs we'll be flying somewhat over 90 nm before there is another airport in sight. And it wouldn't do any good, even if we decided to fly some kind of dogleg. There just aren't any airports of consequence which are any closer. The one which we will spot, some distance to the left of our course, is the Akron-Washington County Airport (Colorado). From there it's another 100 nm or so to North Platte, but at least there are two lighted airports more or less on our course, one called Wray, most likely unattended at this hour, and one called Imperial (Nebraska) which is served by an FSS.

Shortly after passing it, North Platte's lights should start to appear right over the nose of the airplane. By now, of course, we have left that area of unlimited visibilities, and the lights of cities may at first appear as just a glow, becoming more distinct as we get closer.

If we'd have preferred to fly over somewhat less desolate country we could, after passing Akron-Washington, have headed somewhat more northerly and picked up a major highway, I-80, which, along a slightly curved track, would have led us directly to North Platte.

But after that the road dips south and there are no meaningful ground features for a while. We'll be passing two lighted airports, Broken Bow and Burwell (Nebraska). Both are about 12 or 15 miles to the right of our course. Neither is controlled and the chance that someone is manning the Unicom at this time of night is slim indeed. Therefore, if we did have to use an airport like that, we have no way of knowing what the runway surface conditions are.

By the way, let's not be surprised if we are looking for what is supposed to be an airport with lighted runways and all we can see by whatever light is available is the dark line which represents the runway, but no lights. What happens quite often in the winter is that smaller airports will plow their runway, piling the snow on top of the runway lights. The snow then freezes, making it impossible to remove and the lights become useless.

A rather typical experience comes to mind. I was flying toward Lock Haven, Pennsylvania, during a winter night. I had been into its Piper airport many times in the past and was certain that what I was looking at below was it, except that it should have been lighted, but wasn't. I called and the fellow on the Unicom explained about the lights being covered by several feet of snow. But he assured me that the runway itself was clear of snow or ice and that I could land if I felt like it. It was the first time this has ever happened to me, and I didn't feel too happy about the idea of landing in the dead of night on an unlighted runway. Still, I could see it clearly because of the snow cover all around and the landing turned out to be quite routine with no problems whatever.

It should be stressed here that landing at an airport during the winter months, regardless of the time of day or night, should always

We'll go and have a bite to eat while waiting for the airplane to be fueled.

be preceded by communication with someone who knows the condition of the runway surface. If it's a controlled airport, talking to the tower will automatically bring the needed information. If it's an airport served by an FSS, they too will provide that information. But if it's an uncontrolled airport with no one manning a Unicom, extreme caution should be exercised. Runways, even if they have been cleared of all meaningful snow accumulations, tend to be slick, especially at night, and the braking action may be too poor to get the airplane to stop by the time it reaches the end of the runway.

Airport operators will test the braking action by driving cars or trucks up and down the runway. The report, at airports providing some type of two-way communication, usually is something like: "Braking action poor (fair, good) reported by a car (truck or occasionally a Bonanza, DC-3 or other type of aircraft)" Unless the braking action is said to be good, the pilot wanting to land should make the equivalent of a short-field landing, no matter the length of the runway, and, after touching down, should use his brakes rather gingerly. If brakes are applied with too much pressure and one wheel happens to hit a slick spot on the runway, it may result in a ground loop or, at best, serious difficulties with retaining control of the direction of movement.

Never, except in an unavoidable emergency, should a landing be attempted on a snow-covered runway, unless the pilot is quite certain that that snow cover is very thin. Several inches of snow, especially wet snow, tend to reduce the ability of the airplane to roll on the ground and, depending on the speed at the instant of touchdown, the plane could easily tip over onto its nose, breaking the nosewheel and causing serious propeller damage.

From now on the airports will start to appear in more frequent succession. O'Neill, Gurney, Sioux Falls and Worthington and a whole bunch of others while we continue straight on toward Minneapolis, arriving there at about 20 or so minutes past two in the morning.

What we have described in these pages is a straight-line flight with no attention paid to how we would manage to navigate. So maybe we should take a look and see how close we could actually come to flying this straight line.

The Victor Airways would serve us reasonably well part of the time, but between Farmington and Colorado Springs and between Colorado Springs and North Platte they do call for some rather considerable deviation from the straight line.

Leaving Phoenix (PHX) we would take V-95 to Winslow (INW) and from there continue on V-95 to Farmington (FMN). This second leg which is 166 nm long, would require us to fly at 11,300 feet or higher in order to assure reception from the appropriate VORs. (The MEAs are 10,000 on the first leg and 13,000 on the second.)

From Farmington there is no airway that even resembles a straight line to Colorado Springs (COS). V-95 goes to Gunnison (GUC) with an MEA of 16,100 feet and, with no lower reception altitude listed, it is doubtful that we could maintain radio contact much below that altitude. After GUC the airway turns right toward Kiowa (IOC) and some 25 miles or so before reaching IOC we could turn either north toward Denver (DEN) or south toward COS. Again the MEAs and MRAs are above 16,000 feet (16,200 to be exact), which is, of course, out of the question unless we have oxygen on board.

An alternate airway from FMN would be V-210 to Alamosa (ALS) where the MEA and MRA is 14,800 feet, and then from there to the Gosip Intersection (MEA 14,000, MRA 13,600), and at the intersection we could then turn left and follow V-19 to Pueblo (PUB) and from there V-81 to COS.

The second choice is 14 nm longer than the first, but neither would be much better than flying the straight line from Farmington to Colorado Springs, always assuming that there is enough moonlight or starlight to permit us to be able to see the ground. If that is not the case, we couldn't hope to safely fly from FMN to COS, regardless of which route we might want to choose, unless we have sufficient oxygen on board to permit us to fly at least 15,500 feet high which would keep us within approximately 1,000 feet of the highest peak anywhere in the area.

For some reason, though the area is criss-crossed with airways, there is not one that goes directly from COS to Akron-Washington (AKO). They either take us right smack through the Denver TCA which could lead to unnecessary delays, or they detour far to the east. On the other hand, if we climb up high enough (and, after all, we took off from an airport with an elevation in excess of 6,000 feet) we ought to be able to maintain the appropriate outbound radial of the COS VOR until we are able to pick up AKO. But we must, of course, remember that the reception distance of VORs is determined by our altitude above the ground (agl) and not above sea level (msl), so we might have to get up to, say, 11,500 feet, depending on the quality of our VOR receivers.

After passing AKO the airways will again serve pretty well. V-80 goes straight to North Platte (LBF) and from there V-148 takes us via O'Neill (ONL), Sioux Falls (FSD) and Redwood Falls (RWF) direct into Minneapolis (MSP) with only a slight deviation from the straight line. Along all of this part of the route the MRAs are low enough to permit us to select whatever altitude we feel comfortable with.

In closing it might be appropriate to mention again the importance of staying in contact with the FSSs along the way in order to constantly check and recheck the weather ahead. This is always good practice but in the winter the weather has a habit of moving with surprising rapidity. As a result, forecasts are even less reliable than during other times of the year. The trick is to check the *current* weather ahead and to either side of the selected route and to keep track of changes which would be indicative of movement. It wouldn't do to have to tangle with clouds, snow showers or, worst of all, freezing rain. The rapidity with which ice can build up on the leading edges of the wing and tail surfaces and around all manner of protrusions is quite startling, and with all outside being in darkness, we might fail to notice it until the airplane starts to fly sluggishly, which is a bit late.

In this context, it is a good idea to carry one of those high-powered spotlights which can be plugged into the cigarette lighter and throw a beam some 15 or 20 feet. If we find ourselves flying in an area where there appears to be a fair amount of moisture in the air, keep checking the leading edges of the wing every few minutes. It may play hell with our night vision, but that's a lot less worrisome than ice.

And if we do detect ice, most likely the smartest thing would be to head for the nearest airport. Unless we are certain of either much warmer or much colder temperatures at a level, either higher or lower, at which we feel we can safely operate, gambling with the chance that the ice buildup will diminish or at least stop, is a lousy gamble indeed.

Chapter 14
TEB to ZZV

It was raining in New York but I was due in St. Louis the next day and the rain was forecast to stop within the next few hours. Frontal passage had been shortly after five in the afternoon and the friendly voice at the FSS had seemed confident that the sky would be clear by midnight. Even now, with the precipitation still covering most of New Jersey and Pennsylvania, ceilings were said to be around 5,000 feet with visibilities five or better at every reporting station. The one less than inviting feature was the winds-aloft forecast which talked about velocities of 15 and 20 knots right out of the west.

Well, hell, the Centurion is a fast airplane and a 20-knot head-wind would only cut about 12.5 percent off the ground speed.

So I checked out of the hotel, stuffed my junk into the rented Chevrolet and drove out to Teterboro where the Centurion was supposed to be fueled and ready to go. The drive was unpleasant to put it mildly. The rain was still pouring down and Route 3 was full of puddles with passing cars and trucks precipitating veritable water-falls on my windshield. The sky was pitch black without a trace of a star, much less a moon, and, frankly, I was beginning to think that my optimistic weather briefer should have looked out of the window instead of at the reports fed to him by the National Weather Service.

Oh well, maybe it would get better.

I drove the car onto the apron and under the mercifully high wing of the Centurion and managed to stash my stuff without getting soaked. I then drove to the FBO office, signed the fuel bill, returned

The Centurion is a fast airplane and a 20-knot headwind would only cut about 12.5 percent off the ground speed.

the key to the car and gratefully accepted a ride in one of the airport cars back to my airplane.

While I taxied out and went through the usual runup routine a Gulfstream II, two Learjets and a Falcon 20 landed one after the other, their landing lights turning the pouring rain into a curtain of sliver-white streamers.

"Teterboro Tower, Cessna Six Seven Two Three Five ready for takeoff.

"Cessna Two Three Five cleared for immediate takeoff. JetStar on final."

"Two Three Five rolling."

The Centurion, apparently unaware that it wasn't an amphibian, accelerated through the inches of water on the runway, then lifted its nose and headed into black nothingness. Knowing that somewhere northwest of the airport is a tall broadcast tower which would probably be hard to see in this rain, I continued north (I had taken off from Runway One) until I was certain to have passed it and to be at an altitude at which it would no longer be a problem. Then, leveling just under the floor of the overhanging New York TCA, I turned west and into what I assumed were those 15- or 20-knot headwinds.

All in all I can't say that I was particularly comfortable. The rain made a ferocious drumming racket on the windscreen, it was bumpy as hell and, except for a few sparse lights on the ground, I might just has well have been sitting inside an ink bottle. On top of everthing else, water was beginning to seep through the door seal and drip onto my leg and run down into my shoe. Thanks a lot!

I tuned the Number Two nav receiver to the Solberg omni and set the 055-degree radial with the OBS, swearing at avionics manufacturers who made the knobs so small that, in turbulence, your hand kept slipping off them. As the needle began to move toward the center I knew that I was about to get out from under the TCA and I cranked the trim back for a comfortable cruise-climb to a hopefully smoother altitude. The ceiling was supposed to be at 5,000 which would be about 5,500 msl and I figured I should at least be able to get up to 4,500.

Well, I got up there all right, but not for long. There was no way to tell where the real ceiling was, but there was all kinds of scud floating around and time and again the tell-tale green and red halos would suddenly envelop my wingtips. And, for that matter, it wasn't any smoother, so I dropped back down to 3,000 which I knew to be

The Centurion lifted off, its nose heading into black nothingness.

high enough not to hit anything, and at least I could be reasonably certain not to suddenly find myself in a big mess of clouds.

With the other nav radio tuned to 110.2, the East Texas VOR, I engaged the autopilot and the VOR coupler and decided to let the airplane do its thing without my help while I scrounged around for the appropriate chart because it seemed to be about time to find out how fast or slow I was actually going. But, considering my altitude, I guess I was still a bit far because the OFF flag kept popping up and I had to disconnect the coupler again, letting the autopilot, a Century I with no heading hold, keep me on course as best as it could.

By twisting the knob on the Number Two OBS I found that I was just crossing the zero-degree radial of Solberg which, as best as I could make out by the illumination from the dome light, put me a little over 40 nautical miles east of the East Texas VOR. Knowing the terrain in this part of the country to be relatively flat, I was using my Jeppesens as there seemed to be no cause to fight with the expanse of a Sectional.

I turned off the dome light after checking the time—8:42 p.m.—and sat back and waited for the OFF flag to get lost, indicating that the East Texas VOR was finally coming in solid. It took a while, probably seeming a lot longer than it actually was because I was getting impatient, a typical reaction when flying at night, and when it did finally lock on the needle jumped all the way to the left peg. I made a 30-or-so degree course correction to the left and swore out loud, because now I still wouldn't be able to tell the ground speed. Right now a DME would have been nice, but at two grand or more, it just had never been in the budget.

Slowly, ever so slowly, the needle began to creep toward the center and, getting impatient, I adjusted the OBS, centered the needle and found myself on the 248-degree bearing to the station. In other words, I had been drifting considerably to the north. Now I could couple the autopilot again and let it take care of adjusting our heading to whatever direction the wind was blowing from.

By the time the flag finally flipped from TO to FROM the clock read 9:01. It had taken 19 minutes to fly those 40 nm, though, considering the dogleg, it was probably more like 43 or 44 nm. Anyway, even at that, I was moving along at barely 140 knots while the TAS at my altitude and power setting was more like 165 knot. I therefore had to assume that I was fighting a 25-knot headwind component. It was therefore time, after adjusting the OBS to the 261-degree radial from East Texas, the course to Harrisburg, to start doing a little arithmetic.

The total distance from Teterboro to St. Louis is 771 nm. Assuming no more doglegs and no change in the wind, that would take five and a half hours at my current 140 knots. I had started out with 89 usable gallons of fuel, and estimated that at this moment I was burning about 14 gph. That meant that I could fly six hours and 22 minutes until fuel exhaustion, or five hours and 22 minutes if I were to stick to my personal rule of never flying at night with less than one hour's worth of fuel remaining in the tanks. A one-man argument ensued; should I plan to fudge by those eight minutes, or should I stop somewhere, say Indianapolis, and get the tanks topped off?

Oh, what the heck. Let's wait and see. Maybe the wind will die down, or may be I'll be able to climb up higher where I'll be burning less fuel. As a matter of fact, I'd damn well better be able to climb a bit higher with those mountains between Harrisburg and Pittsburgh creasing the Pennsylvania landscape to around 3,000 feet or more in some places.

That reminded me. Where the hell was Harrisburg anyway? It seemed as if I had been flying for hours but the needle in the Number Two OBI, tuned to Harrisburg, still refused to budge. So far the autopilot was still stubbornly hanging on to the ETX radial, but not for long. The red edge of the OFF flag kept popping up intermittently. And then, just as it popped into place for good, HAR came in and I switched the coupler from the Number One to the Number Two nav receiver and the autopilot calmly continued me on my way to HAR.

The turbulence had by now abated somewhat and even though it was still raining, the rain, too, had slackened and I begin to feel reasonably confident that I'd be able to make St. Louis without a fuel stop after all.

Coming closer to Harrisburg I suddenly saw a couple of stars through that blackness above and I was just about to pick up the mike and call Harrisburg radio for some current weather farther along my route, when some other pilot got ahead of me.

"Harrisburg Radio, Comanche Eight Zero One Two Pop, over."

"One Two Pop, this is Harrisburg. Go ahead."

"Harrisburg Radio, One Two Pop, two zero west at three thousand, reporting heavy rain showers with the base of the clouds apparently around three thousand five hundred, occasionally lower. What are you reporting at Harrisburg? Over."

"One Two Pop, thanks for the pilot report. Current Harrisburg weather, fifty-five hundred overcast with occasional breaks, visibility eight, light rain showers, wind two three zero degrees at one five, gusting to three zero, over."

"Thank you, Harrisburg. What about farther east, Philadelphia, New York?"

"Stand by one." Pause. "One Two Pop, Philadelphia is reporting one thousand overcast, visibility four in heavy rain, and New York is down too, fifteen hundred overcast, visibility one and a half."

There was a short pause with the Comanche pilot apparently trying to figure out what to do. When he came on again he asked to file IFR and then went ahead with his flight plan to Westchester County Airport.

Damn! That weather he'd been reporting 20 west of Harrisburg sure didn't sound particularly inviting. If that 3,500 he'd reported for the cloud bases was msl, and it quite obviously was, then there would be awfully little room between those bases and all those rocks around Johnstown. Well, if it got too bad I could always turn back and wait it out in Harrisburg.

The lights of Harrisburg passed below and at 9:32 I was over the VOR. Thirty-one minutes to fly 65 nm. That figured out to a ground speed of 126 knots. At that rate there wasn't a chance of making it all the way to St. Louis. Well, after all, there are hundreds of airports along the way, and a lot of big ones like Pittsburgh or Dayton or Indianapolis where they'd surely have 24-hour service.

The autopilot was now locked onto the 282-degree radial from Harrisburg and suddenly the rain stopped and above was a whole huge bunch of stars. Boy, it sure would be nice to get up there on top of all this mess.

"Harrisburg Radio, Cessna Six Seven Two Three Five, over."

"Two Three Five, Harrisburg. Go ahead."

"Do you have any reports on the tops of this stuff?"

"We've got one that's nearly an hour old now. Tops one zero west of Johnstown two five thousand reported by a Mitsubishi."

Okay, so I'd have to forget about climbing on top. "How about the current Pittsburgh weather?"

"Pittsburgh is reporting two thousand broken, five thousand overcast, visibility eight in drizzle. Occasional lightning observed north. Over."

Oh, so now we've got a thunderstorm on top of everything else. "Two Three Five, thanks."

"Harrisburg altimeter two niner seven three."

"Two Three Five."

I adjusted the altimeter, finding that I was actually cruising at 3,300 and I figured I might as well stay there. After all, being within 3,000 feet of the ground I could legally fly anywhere I wanted to.

The stars above disappeared. Below the headlights of the cars on the Pennsylvania Turnpike veered off to the left, leaving the terrain ahead mostly black except for a few occasional lights here and there. According to the Jeppesen it was 83 nm to Johnstown and according to the Sectional which I now had spread out on the seat to my right, if I could make it past Johnstown I'd have most of the mountains behind me.

It was raining again, not hard, but steady. I switched tanks and turned the cockpit lights to low in order to better be able to see outside. I figured that as long as there were lights ahead and below I could safely fly on, knowing that there could not be any obstacle between me and those lights.

Suddenly there was a huge, crooked bolt of lightning ahead and to the right, for a split second illuminating the whole area. But that split second was sufficient to imprint the picture on my mind. The ceiling was quite a ways above me, the ground was a comfortable distance below. And then there was another such bolt of lightning, this one right in front of me and I instinctively changed direction to the left and disconnected the autopilot coupler.

The OBI needle moved off center, but so what? I damn well wasn't going to fly into whatever lay straight ahead. Lightning scares me.

I had been flying along the bottom edge of the Detroit Sectional and now I dug out the Washington one to get a good look at the terrain farther south. In that direction the next VOR was St. Thomas and all the terrain around there seemed to be around 2,300 and 2,500, which wasn't too bad as long as the clouds stayed up where they belonged. I switched the radio to 115.0, the St. Thomas frequency and was glad to see it come in right away, so I recoupled the autopilot and let it struggle with the bumpiness which was gradually getting worse again. I guessed those surface winds they had been reporting in Harrisburg were burbling over those mountain ridges below and stirring things up pretty good.

There was more lightning, but it kept off to my right, so I tried to ignore it. At three minutes off 10 o'clock I was over St. Thomas with the lights of the Pennsylvania Turnpike curving back and forth to my right, occasionally disappearing where the road went through one or another of those tunnels.

Being now south of my intended course, the next VOR in more or less the right direction would be Indian Head, 65 nm distant along the 280-degree radial from St. Thomas. According to the Jeppesen the minimum en-route altitude was 5,000 feet, but on the Sectional (I was now getting onto the Cincinnati Sectional) the highest place I could find was 2,994 feet, just north of the Indian Head VOR. I trimmed the nose up a bit, figuring I'd see if I could stay in the clear at 4,000.

There hadn't been any more lightning except at a considerable distance to the north and I began to hope that, with any kind of luck, maybe I had left the worst of the weather behind me by now.

At 4,000 I was still in the clear and decided to continue up some more, but moments later there was some low-hanging scud and I resigned myself to settling for four.

By the time I crossed Indian Head the ground speed had dropped by another three or four knots, and it was then that I began to seriously consider that I might be better off on the ground. Not only was I burning more fuel than I had planned on, I also found that I was getting increasingly weary from constantly being bounced around, and at this rate of progress it simply was going to take forever to get anywhere at all.

Once the idea had taken hold I wondered why I hadn't simply put down in Harrisburg and saved myself the aggravation of the last hour or so. Well, it was too late for that, so on came the dome light and I began to search on the charts for the next logical airport. I called Indian Head, which is served by the Morgantown FSS and asked for the Pittsburgh weather. That took care of Pittsburgh. They still had thunderstorms and now the visibility was way down in heavy rain. I asked about Wheeling, which, according to the Sectional, seemed like a logical place.

"Wheeling Ohio Country, four thousand overcast, visibility five, light rain."

Okay, Wheeling, here I come. I made the necessary course correction and, so far unable to get the Wheeling VOR, tuned to Bellaire, only a few miles south of it. It came in fine and by using the bearing from a present position to Bellaire, I figured roughly the right direction to fly to get to Wheeling. It took a while but eventually Wheeling did come in and soon afterwards I was able to raise Wheeling Tower on 118.1 and was cleared to land as soon as I told them that I had the airport in sight.

I had never before landed there, but had figured that there must be a motel somwhere nearby. That tuned out to be wishful thinking. The nearest RON was in the town itself, some 12 miles away, and there were neither rental cars nor taxis at the airport. Granted, I probably could have called one from town, but, being told what that would cost, I discarded that idea. Some local type suggested I fly on to Zanesville. "They've got a Holiday Inn and a Howard Johnson practically right on the airport."

I looked at the chart. Zanesville was bout 60 nm west of Wheeling. Okay, another 60 miles won't kill me.

I checked the weather. Fifteen overcast, visibility eight, light rain. Hummm. The Zanesville airport is at an elevation of 900 feet, meaning that the overcast is at 2,400 msl. On the other hand, there is a straight highway leading directly from Wheeling, the town that is, to Zanesville. The Wheeling airport itself sits atop a kind of bluff overlookng the Ohio River, some 400 or so feet above the town. Since the ceiling here was still ample, I assumed that it must drop quite rapidly somewhere to the west and I decided that the thing to do would be to fly down over the town and then pick up that highway and stay over it all the way to Zanesville.

I checked the chart for obstructions along that route. There was a whole bunch in the Wheeling area itself and then two more north of the highway around some town called Saint Clairsville, and farther on a real lulu, also north of the highway, reaching up to 2,349 feet msl—obviously one to be avoided.

Anyway, there wasn't much point in continuing to sit around in this depressingly deserted airport, so I climbed back into the Centurion, took off and once over the Ohio River, dropped down towards the lights of the city of Wheeling, West Virginia. The highway leading west out of town came into view and I positioned myself slightly to the south of it, figuring that no matter how low I would have to fly, on that side there would be no sudden towers sticking up into the sky.

And it wasn't long until, in order to stay clear of the clouds, I was tooling along at barely six or seven hundred feet above the highway.

It took a little over 25 minutes until the Zanesville rotating beacon came into view. Zanesville is an uncontrolled airport, but there is an FSS on the field and I was given the active runway and asked for a report on the weather.

Ten minutes later I was in my room at the Holiday Inn, and glad to be where I was. The next morning the weather was CAVU and stayed that way all the way to St. Louis.

In retrospect I am perfectly willing to admit that undertaking this flight was not one of the most intelligent things I have ever done. As best as I can figure, I had traveled some 400 actual miles in order to cover a 350-mile straight-line distance and, including that half hour on the ground at Wheeling, it had taken me just short of four hours to get there. I had, as I found out the next day, burned an outrageous 52 gallons of fuel as a result of the low altitude and a higher-than-normal power setting to overcome the headwind component.

All that time I had operated at an altitude which meant that in the event of some kind of engine trouble I wouldn't have had the slightest chance of finding a place to land. Also, it would have been intelligent to top the tanks at Wheeling instead of taking off without knowing exactly what I had left. After all, if that attempt of getting to Zanesville had turned out to be a bummer, I might have been forced to detour to some heaven only knows what other place, a situation which would have been a lot less hair-raising with 80-some gallons of fuel in the wings.

But then, I guess, all of us at one time or another take stupid chances. At least, I don't think I know anyone who never has, and I'm not sure that I would want to. Living one's life without ever taking a chance must be rather dull.

Chapter 15
Landing at Yucca Valley

There was a time, it's quite a few years ago now, that I was living right off the runway at the airport at Yucca Valley, California, some 20 miles north of Palm Springs. I guess I was technically the airport manager, even though there wasn't much to manage, but the one thing I did have to do was to make sure that the airport lights got turned on before dark, and off again when it got light. Actually, they were supposed to go on and off automatically, but half the time that timer they were attached to went on the blink, and one had to turn them on and off manually.

I was flying a 150-hp Cardinal in those days, an airplane that quite undeservedly had gotten itself a bad reputation because a bunch of dummies, who thought that, being a Cessna, it should land like any other Cessna, had made lousy landings and busted a bunch of nose wheels. But that's another story.

One time I had taken the Cardinal up to Lake Tahoe where there was a convention of the various California aviation associations, and when it was all over I decided to fly home that very night. It was a beautiful night, no weather anywhere, and I felt wide awake and in great shape, so why not?

I took off from Truckee-Tahoe airport which sits in a sort of circular valley surrounded by some pretty high mountains. There was no moon, so I simply circled over the airport until I got enough altitude to see the lights on the far side of the mountains, which meant that I was now high enough to get safely over the tops.

This was familiar territory, and I knew that a straight-line route from Lake Tahoe to Yucca Valley was out of the question. Not only would that take me for hours on end right over the tops of the Sierra Nevada which includes the highest mountain in the U.S. except for Alaska (Mt. Whitney, 14,495 feet), but also leads into a labyrinth of restricted and prohibited areas in the China Lake and Edwards Air Force Base region where they are not too terribly hospitable toward light aircraft. And, if that weren't enough, there are virtually no airports anywhere, and I knew I'd have to refuel somewhere en route.

The sensible thing to do, and this was one of my sensible nights, was to head southwest toward the San Joaquin Valley which is lousy with airports all the way from Sacramento down to Bakersfield, then refuel in Bakersfield and head east toward Palmdale, Apple Valley and around Mount Gorgonio into Yucca Valley. That last part was going to be pretty lonely and desolate, but I had flown it many times and it had long stopped bothering me.

There is little to tell about the flight itself, except that by the time I landed in Bakersfield, I realized that I was a lot more tired than I had thought I was. Still, I refueled, took off again, crossed the southern extremities of the Sierra Nevada, saw Palmdale in the distance, headed toward it, overflew it and continued on toward my destination. Everything was fine until I got close enough to the Yucca Valley to see the lights of the town and should have been able to see the runway lights of the airport which is located at its east end. No airport. It just wasn't there.

First I thought that I must have made some stupid mistake, and that this wasn't Yucca Valley after all, but that just couldn't be. Everything was where it was supposed to be, everything, that is, except the airport.

And then it dawned on me. The lights hadn't come on. Damn! Tired as I was, I certainly was in no mood to fly down to Palm Springs and then try to figure out whether to rent a car and drive home, or stay down there in one of those fancy overpriced motels.

It was a dark night. Clear, but no moon and the stars didn't do an awful lot of good. What to do?

I circled the area which I knew contained the airport. I could barely see my house and clearly see the lights from the restaurant which is located off the west end of the runway, and the drive-in theatre beyond. I knew exactly where the runway should be, except that I couldn't see it. I had landed there hundreds of times, day and night, and I felt confident that, if I flew the familiar pattern over familiar landmarks, I'd be able to line myself up with the runway, even if I couldn't see it, and that I should be able to get down low enough to get some kind of use out of my landing lights. The trick was not to get rattled and to do it all quite calmly and as slowly as I could make that bird go without its dropping out from under me.

I circled three more times at a safe altitude, just to make quite sure that I knew exactly where everything was. (In case you wonder, there was no point in calling on the Unicom, because it was in my house and my wife was in Los Angeles that week.)

I flew the pattern, probably the most perfect pattern I have flown since the days when there was an instructor in the seat next to me, watched the altimeter carefully. The field elevation at Yucca Valley is 3,220 feet and before starting down I had asked Palm Springs for the current altimeter setting. I turned base, dropped down lower and used the lights from the restaurant and the drive-in theatre on the far side of the airport as guide. I turned final, dropped down still lower, 3,250, 3,240... And then there it was. A grey glow as the landing lights picked up the grey hard surface of the runway, right straight ahead and below. It was just the barest glow, but it was solid grey, no bushes or rocks or anything else that might throw a shadow. I pulled the throttle all the way back and felt the wheels touching down. It'll be a long time until I make another such perfectly greased-on landing. Beautiful!

I taxied to the far end of the runway, turned on the lights, just in case some other poor soul should decide to come in there during what was left of the night, then taxied to my house and went to bed.

It worked, but I'd sure hate to ever have to do it again. And the only reason why it had worked at all was that I knew that airport so very well.

Chapter 16
Waco to Houston in the Rain

The airplane was a pre-PC Mooney with a slight list to port, meaning that it required constant light pressure on the right rudder pedal or correction to the right with the alierons in order to produce a semblance of straight-ahead flight. Otherwise it was a nice little airplane with a healthy engine which kept humming away with nary a cough and dual navcoms which had been guiding us fairly reliably on an extended two-week tour around most of the country. My passenger was a young actor and former world-champion skydiver who repeatedly assured me that he preferred jumping out of airplanes to flying in them. We were flying from one city to another for radio and television interviews to promote a new television series about general aviation which subsequently, despite our efforts, faded into oblivion.

On this day we had done our thing at several broadcast stations in Dallas and had flown to Waco for a quick bite to eat before going in to Houston.

So far the weather, though overcast, had been quite good, but a visit to the FSS in Waco produced the information that the ceilings between Waco and Houston were hovering around the 1,000 to 1,500-foot level with reasonable visibilities below except for areas of light to moderate rain showers.

Though it didn't sound particularly inviting, it did sound flyable. Today I would probably have filed instruments for that short 160-nm flight, but this was some years ago when I didn't have the ticket, so it was either VFR or RON. I forget now why I apparently felt that it was important for us to get to Houston that night, but I assume that there was a fairly good reason. Anyway, we decided to go.

Waco itself was amply VFR with ceilings above 3,000 feet and sufficient breaks in the overcast to give us a frequent look at the moon and stars. But we couldn't have been airborne for more than a few minutes when the ceiling did drop down to a level which gave us barely 1,000 feet clearance between it and the ground.

Now, there aren't any mountains or other major obstacles between Waco and Houston except for five tall transmission towers, one south of Waco, one west of Houston's Hobby Airport and the other three way off course to the west, one south of Temple and the other two in Austin. West of Temple there is also a small horseshoe-shaped restricted area, but none of this should present a problem, because the straight route from Waco via College Station to Houston was far to the east of all of it.

At least that's how I figured it. In practice it turned out quite differently. The first thing that happened was that as soon as I had leveled off at something like 1,500 or 1,600 msl, which kept us barely 1,000 feet above the ground and at the same time reasonably clear of the clouds directly above us, we hit a fairly juicy rainshower which effectively blocked our view of the ground straight ahead, and I turned several degrees to the right to stay clear of it by constantly keeping some lights on the ground in view.

This kind of flying isn't bad if there is a well-traveled highway or something like that to follow. But when there isn't, you find yourself constantly making corrections to the right or left, simply in order to retain some semblance of visual contact with whatever lights there are on the ground. After a while we did pick up a highway, but by this time I wasn't too sure which one it was and since it, too, led into another rather heavy rainshower, I reluctantly abandoned it and kept flying from one batch of lights to another, realizing by now that I was drifting farther and farther to the west since everything to the east and southeast was one black sodden mess.

I probably should have paid more attention to my OBI, because when I suddenly did decide to see what it had to say, I found that we were on the 220-degree radial from Temple, which certainly put us one hell of a long distance to the west of where we should have been.

Just then I spotted all kinds of lights to my left and turned sharply toward them, hoping that by flying in an easterly direction I might be able to get us back onto some resemblance of what should have been our course.

It worked for a while. I crossed several highways, one of which seemed to lead in the direction in which I wanted to go, and I stubbornly held my heading until another batch of rain got in the way and I had to quickly decide whether to turn north or south. Well, Houston being obviously south of wherever we were at that moment, I turned to the right, flying straight south for a while, and then finding again that I had to keep turning more and more southwesterly in order to maintain ground contact.

Through all of this, both my passenger and I kept staring into the dark ahead, searching for possible obstructions to be avoided. Time and again I had had to drop lower to say out of the bottom of the overcast, and, according to the Sectional, there were quite a number of obstructions of one kind or another, sticking up high enough to present a possible problem. I'm sure the chart was right and I'm sure they were there somewhere, but we never did see any of them.

After a while I saw a lighted airport near some sort of highway and was briefly tempted to land and try again in the morning, and I probably should have, but I didn't. I had no idea which airport that was. It wasn't a big one and now, looking at the chart and trying to reconstruct where we most likely were scooting around right then, it might have been Georgetown, some distance north of Austin.

Anyway, I overflew it and was by now heading east again, this time tuned to Austin with the OBI telling me that I was somewhere north of that VOR. As best as I could guess, and I never did have a chance to really study the charts, what with us being as close to the ground as we were, we were now nearly as far from Houston as we had been when we started this flight, only instead of it being south-south-east of us, it was now more or less straight east.

I tried to hold a heading of roughly 90 degrees for as long as the showers let me; then headed south for a while, hoping to be able to pick up the 090-degree radial from Austin which points just about straight to the northend of the city of Houston. I figured that if I ever picked up the lights of the city, it wouldn't be too difficult to get to the southside of town and find Hobby airport.

I also talked to Austin and learned that Houston was currently reporting 2,000 scattered, 4,000 overcast, five miles visibility and intermittent rainshowers to the north. Well, at least it was VFR. After all this flying around I would have hated to arrive there only to be told that it was IFR. The forecast called for no significant change.

I really don't have a very clear idea of our exact route of flight. Using my rather vivid memory of it and the charts, I have tried to reconstruct it as best as I could, and to show it in the accompanying illustration.

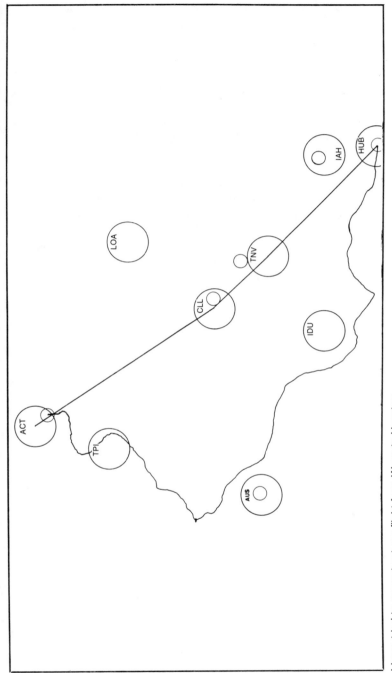

I have tried to reconstruct our flight from Waco to Houston.

The fact is that the ceiling never did lift until we arrived within about 10 miles of Houston. The fact is also that it took us close to three hours to get from Waco to Houston, a distance which, flown in a straight line, should have been covered in an hour plus possibly a few minutes.

It goes without saying that we arrived safely, since I am sitting here writing about it. There is also little doubt that making this flight was a rather stupid decision. After the first 15 or 20 minutes I should have turned back and stayed the night in Waco. Granted, the next day the weather wasn't much better, but, at least, we'd have had daylight which would have simplified matters considerably.

Of all the night flights which I can remember, I always think of this one as the dumbest, as the one which could quite easily have turned out to be the last flight of my life. There is really no excuse for a VFR pilot to do what I did that night. In that kind of weather, either file IFR or stay on the ground. After all, no matter how important it might seem to be to get to where one wants to go, there is no point at all in getting there dead.

Chapter 17
A Summer Night in the Mountains

A year or two ago I found myself one afternoon in Colorado Springs, having finished a series of business appointments, and with my next such appointment involving lunch in Las Vegas, Nevada. (I was on a research assignment which involved interviewing corporate pilots in various parts of the western U.S.) I was flying a middle-aged Cessna 182 which, I had found out, cruised about 130 knots at a reasonable power setting.

The straight-line distance from Colorado Springs to Las Vegas is about 500 nm, but it's also the kind of country which virtually precludes flying a straight line. Directly west of Colorado Springs the surface elevations reach up into the mid-14,000s and without oxygen I had no intention of flying at such altitudes for the length of time necessary to get to where the colors on my sectional charts lightened from dark brown to a more reasonable tan-yellow.

In addition, the fellow at the FSS felt dutybound to assure me that to make the flight VFR was inadvisable because a front was moving in from Wyoming with the higher mountains west of Denver already obscured, while the last front, which had moved through the day before, had stalled in the Santa Fe area, producing all kinds of thunderstorms and a variety of messy weather.

I asked about Alamosa and Farmington, and he seemed reluctant to admit that both were in pretty good shape with only high clouds and visibilities in the 40s and 50s.

Despite his obvious desire to con me into either filing IFR or staying where I was, I decided to do neither. As far as I am

I was flying a middle-aged Cessna 182.

concerned, IFR in the Rockies is out of the question without oxygen, what with those 16,000-foot-plus MEAs. On the other hand, the appointment in Las Vegas was important because the fellow I was supposed to see was slated to go on a weeklong trip in the company King Air that very next afternoon.

I decided to fly south from Colorado Springs past Pueblo to something that on the charts is identified as the Gosip Intersection (178° from Pueblo and 061° from Alamosa) and then fly from there to Alamosa and on to Farmington. Even though I knew that I could reach Las Vegas with the full fuel on board, I had no intention of playing around with running low, so I would stop in Farmington, have a bite to eat, and then go on, again with full tanks, plus having had a chance to study the weather for the rest of the trip.

It was still light out by the time I took off, and I got across the highest of the various mountain ranges before the last light of day decided to fade out. Except for a 15-or-so-knot headwind and occasionally rather unpleasant turbulence, the flight was uneventful, but I could tell from the streakiness of the high clouds, still picking up the last of the sunlight, that the weather was certainly moving in my direction, and that I'd be best off to get out of this area just as fast as that venerable 182 would take me.

West of Farmington Shiprock represents an unmistakable landmark.

What made the flight memorable was the leg from Farmington to Las Vegas. While the weather west of Farmington was not expected to produce any unpleasant surprises, the reports did indicate that there would most likely be a solid overcast, high enough not to give me any trouble, but, in addition to the fact that there wasn't going to be any moon that night anyway, it would certainly remove any chance of making use of what little light the stars might be willing to provide.

When I took off from Farmington there were still all kinds of stars in the sky and I optimistically decided that the forecast had been wrong as usual, and that it would be a much simpler flight than had been predicted. Well, forecasts for this area and even reports of current weather tend to be rather spotty, with reporting locations being hundreds of miles apart. And this proved to be one of those times which bear this out.

The first unpleasantness came when I tried to climb up to about 12,500 feet after leaving Farmington. The distance from Farmington to Shiprock, which sticks out like an unmistakable landmark, is just under 30 nm, meaning that cruise-climbing at a TAS of 115 knots, I should have covered that distance in about 15 or 16 minutes. Nothing like that happened. It took 21 minutes to get to that hunk of volcanic rock, giving me a ground speed of barely over 85 knots. Conclusion, I was fighting a 30-knot headwind. That was close to 25 percent of my cruising speed and I hadn't even leveled off at the altitude at which I wanted to fly, meaning that it was likely to blow even harder up there.

And right then, straight ahead, there was this sudden flash of light. Well, I had been sort of wondering why it seemed so much blacker straight ahead and to the left than it did to the right. Now I knew. Thunderstorms, a whole bunch of them, doing their usual exciting fireworks-thing right on the route I had wanted to fly and all along for as far as I could see to the left.

So what did all this mean? It meant, either go back to Farmington and forget about that appointment in Las Vegas, or turn right and try to fly around all that mess. It also meant staying low. With that kind of wind, flying at altitude would be the nearest thing to pumping an exercycle: A lot of energy producing no appreciable motion.

Okay, I said to myself, the hell with the airways and the hell with staying within reception distance on one of those few and far between VORs. Let's turn right and stay low. After all, even if I did get the blown slightly off course without being aware of it, it would take a greater genius than mine to miss Lake Powell which lies

It took 21 minutes to get to that hunk of volcanic rock.

across that route like a nest of giant alligators. And one thing I was sure of, no matter how dark it got, I'd sure be able to spot all that water.

Keeping that display of pyrotechnics to my left (and frankly beginning to enjoy the spectacle) I dropped down to within what I figured to be about 1,000 feet of the ground and took up a heading which I assumed to be along the border of Arizona and Utah which I was certain, would take me right over Lake Powell. Though I don't like the idea of flying that low at night, I decided that it really didn't make any difference. With the kind of surface below me, rocks, arroyos, not a flat place within a hundred miles, it really didn't. If that engine should suddenly decide to quit, there wouldn't be a decent place to put the bird down, no matter how high I might be when it happened. And airports? There wasn't one with lights for over 150 nm in the direction in which I was headed.

I can't say that I was terribly relaxed. There was enough light, I really don't know for what source, to permit me to see the ground when I had the instrument lights turned down to an absolute minimum. As a result I found myself peering strenuously into the darkness ahead to make sure that I didn't get too close to some of those rocks which tend to stick out of this high plateau for no apparently good reason.

I'd been hoping for some sort of landmark for some time, not really knowing what it might be, when suddenly there, right in front of me, rose what in the available light looked like Manhattan after it was hit by an atomic bomb. Monument Valley! Keeping one eye tightly shut to not totally destroy my night vision I checked the chart and found that I had traveled slightly over 100 nm since leaving Farmington. It had taken over an hour. Thanks a lot!

Monument Valley is an incredibly spectacular place in the daytime. At night, under the conditions under which I overflew it then, it was eerie. Like a bunch of mis-shapen giants reaching up toward me. Weird. Exciting, but still weird.

But at least one thing was certain. If I was overflying Monument Valley, I certainly couldn't miss Lake Powell, except that there was still a mountain ridge between me and it, with peaks around 8,000 and one of over 10,000 feet. So, wind or no wind, I'd have to climb to a higher altitude until I got past it.

I did, leveling off at just under 9,000 at which point my OBI needle began to react to the Page VOR (PGA) which I knew to be located at the very southern tip of the lake. With the thunderstorms now mostly behind me I made a slight course correction to the south, trying to get onto the 060-degree radial from PGA (the

With the kind of surface below me, rocks, arroyos, not a flat place within a hundred miles, it made little difference how high I was flying.

119

240-degree bearing to PGA) which, according to the chart, would keep me safely south of that 10,388-foot Navajo Mountain peak.

After a while I could just barely make it out to my right and then beyond could see the water of the lake.

Much as I hated to, considering the headwind, I figured that I might as well stay at my altitude, because about 40 nm beyond Page I would be crossing the northern end of the Kaibab Plateau with elevations around 8,000 or so. At its southern end this mountain complex is bordered by the Grand Canyon.

From here on it would be strictly flying a heading and using whatever pilotage was possible with the available light. There simply isn't a usable navaid anywhere unless I was willing to detour far to the north and use Bryce Canyon (BCE), Cedar City (CDC) and then turn south again toward Mormon Mesa (MMM) and Las Vegas (LAS). I figured I was losing enough time with that damn wind, without adding that extra distance. So I hung on to the 250-degree radial from Page for as long as I could pick it up, and after that just used the compass, again figuring that I wasn't very likely to miss the immense expanse of Lake Mead which lay between me and Las Vegas.

For a while there were now breaks in the overcast, and though it didn't help much with the illumination, it did help some, and I could reasonably clearly see the ground beneath me as I was crossing the Kaibab Plateau, clearing it by what I estimated was occasionally less than 500 feet.

I tried like mad to pick up the Grand Canyon or Bryce Canyon VORs, hoping to be able to get some sort of an inkling as to my ground speed, but no luck. Either I was too low or too far away. Anyway, they refused to come in, so I simply kept on flying, and when the ground below dropped down I dropped down with it.

The trouble with this kind of flying is that much of the time you simply haven't got the foggiest notion where you are. Not a landmark anywhere; neither nav receiver bringing in anything resembling a signal. And, while one can usually be reasonably certain that the upper winds will blow for considerable time and distance from one and the same direction, winds this close to the ground have a way of changing frequently and without anything resembling a logical reason. And, of course, the airplane simply goes along with those winds, moving subtly off its course without letting the pilot know what's going on. In daylight one can at least get an inkling by comparing the direction of the nose of the aircraft to the direction in which it is moving across the ground. But at night, barely able to see the ground in the first place, that doesn't work too well.

Flying low over the mountains at night is an eerie experience.

In retrospect it appears that the winds must have shifted to the south while I, expecting them to be more or less northwesterly, had been holding a heading which I expected to eventually bring me toward Lake Mead. The first indication of what was going on was when I idly twiddled with the OBSs on the two nav receivers and suddenly both, Bryce Canyon and Cedar City came in quite strong. It took me only moments to realize that I was way north of my course, because once I got both those needles centered they put me at a spot southeast of one and southwest of the other but way north of where I had expected to be. I was at the intersection of the 150-degree radial from CDC and the 210-degree radial from BCE, which put me right over the southern edge of Zion National Park. What the hell was I doing way up in Utah?

Well, anyway, according to the chart the 225-degree radial from BCE would lead me to Mormon Mesa some distance north of Lake Mead, and from there I'd finally be able to ride the VOR indications all the way to Las Vegas. I made a sharp left turn and promptly lost the signal from BCE, probably because I was way low again, maybe only 1,000 or so feet agl. There came the lights of an airport, ahead and slightly off to my right, into view, and without being certain I assumed it to be St. George. So far so good. I tuned one nav receiver to MMM, figuring that it would have to come in eventually. The only trouble still ahead were two bumps in the ground, one 6,786 and one 7,746 feet high and for some reason I had decided that the right thing to do was to fly between the two.

I was still receiving CDC, though the signal was somewhat intermittent, but the chart said that the 200-degree radial from CDC would put me right between those two bumps and over a road which I could then follow to Mormon Mesa and, if necessary, Las Vegas.

Suddenly I decided, this is ridiculous. I might as well climb to at least 8,000 feet and never mind the wind. At least that would keep me above the highest spot in the immediate vicinity of where I assumed I was. But, surprise! Where had those clouds come from? Just under 7,500 feet there I was suddenly in the clouds and that certainly wasn't what I had had in mind.

So, down again I went and by the time I was back in the clear the signal from CDC had decided to give up the ghost. (You must have realized by now that the nav receivers in this 182 weren't exactly Collins-type quality.) But how I did see the headlights from cars on that road which I was certain was the one I was looking for, and I got right over the top of it and followed it south, vaguely seeing in the darkness those two mountains between which both it and I were snaking our way southwestward.

I had been hoping for some sort of a landmark when suddenly there, right in front of me, like the ruins of Manhattan after an atomic attack, lay Monument Valley.

I kept on flying nearly 500 feet or so above the mountains.

Just then I picked up the signal from MMM and was able to center the needle and fly right to it. Once past it I called Las Vegas, was turned over to Approach Control which didn't shorten the trip any by vectoring me straight south to the east side of Lake Mead in

Having no contact with any anv aid, I searched the ground for recognizable landmarks.

order to keep me out of an area used heavily by the pilot's from Nellis Air Force Base (though I should think that by now they would all be happily in bed).

I could reasonably clearly see the ground below me as I was crossing the Kaibab Plateau.

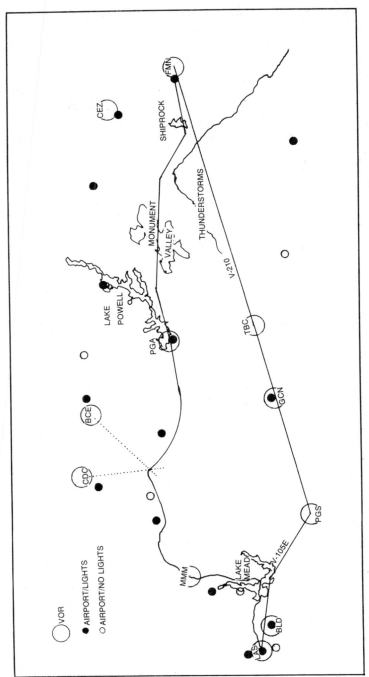

The flight path from Farmington to Las Vegas.

Anyway, though I suddenly realized that I was quite tired and that the amount of fuel left in the airplane, though not critically short, was not exactly fat, I followed instructions and finally managed to get both the tired airplane and the tired pilot safely on the ground at Las Vegas' McCarran Airport.

I have no idea many miles I had flown that night. The straight-line distance from Farmington to Las Vegas is 330 nm which should have taken a bit over two and a half hours. The fact was that it had taken me nearly five hours to cover the distance, and if I did anything right on that whole trip from Colorado Springs, it was the fact that I had stopped in Farmington and, in addition to having a reasonably decent dinner, had the tanks topped off. If I had not done that, figuring that, after all, Las Vegas was easily (well, maybe not easily, but still) within the range of the aircraft, I'd most certainly have run out of fuel somewhere in that mountain wilderness.

Let me add as a postscript. I have flown a great deal in the Rocky Mountains, summer, winter, day and night, and thus have accumulated a fair amount of experience with this kind of flying. Pilots finding themselves in this part of the country for the first time, hailing from places like Kansas or such where anything 10 feet high is considered a mountain, don't try it at night! It's tough enough in the daytime!

Epilogue

I don't know whether this book will have the effect of encouraging the reader to fly into the night behind a single engine, or if it tends to discourage him instead. Most likely, it will do one thing for some and something else for others. There is no right or wrong way of deciding about night flight. The pilot who refuses to fly single-engine after dark is not a coward, and the one who does fly when the sun is busy lighting up the other side of the globe, is neither a fool nor a hero.

Personally, I very much like night flying, when winds are usually fairly calm and the air, more often than not, is smooth. It may seem strange, considering the lack of anything visual, but there is a strange beauty up there at night, a wonderful calm such as is rarely possible to experience at any other time.

It was on a calm night like that, flying from west to east, that suddenly a strange light appeared straight ahead. What was it? The landing light of another aircraft flying toward me? A UFO? Was it moving or did it remain still? It seemed to do neither, but it grew in size quite suddenly and rapidly and I threw the airplane into a sharp left turn in an effort to take evasive action, expecting some huge airplane to momentarily pass at my right.

No airplane passed; the light rose and grew and turned out to be friend rather than foe. I had taken evasive action to avoid the moon which, rising above an odd crevice in the horizon, had fooled me for just a moment.

I think I'll go out to the airport. It looks as if it's going to be a perfect night.

Or on another night, calm and smooth, flying from east to west across Nevada. It was a black moonless night with only the stars above to keep me company.

Quite suddenly and without any warning it was daylight, or nearly so, everything being brightly illuminated by some strange glow to the north. I don't know how long it lasted, seconds maybe, surely less than a minute. I had no idea what it was. There was no weather, no turbulence, and within moments everything was black and calm again as it had been.

The next day the papers reported a nuclear test explosion in the Nevada desert. I had not been close, had been in no danger, and maybe the light I had seen had not been as bright as I thought it to be. Still, it was an eerie experience which I'll never forget.

I've just had to turn on the light in my study. The sun is setting out west, turning the tops of the Sangre de Cristo mountains outside my window the orange-red which gave them their name. I think I'll say Good Night now and go to the airport. It looks as if it's going to be a perfect night.

Glossary

Glossary of Terms and Abbreviations

ACT—Waco, Texas.

ADF—Automatic direction finder, a cockpit instrument using low-frequency navigation aids and standard broadcast stations to indicate the position of the aircraft relative to them.

agl—above ground level.

AKO—Akron, Colorado.

ALS—Alamosa, Colorado.

altimeter setting—The altimeter setting in relation to the prevailing barometric pressure at a given location. In aviation-radio communications usually referred to simply as "altimeter."

ANX—The Napoleon VOR near Kansas City, Missouri.

area navigation—A means of navigating along a direct line from one point to another, using a combination of navigation receiver, DME and a course-line computer which enables the pilot to electronically "move" a ground-based navigation aid from its actual location to another location. Such electronically relocated navigation aids are referred to as waypoints.

Arrow—A single-engine retractable-gear aircraft manufactured by Piper Aircraft Corporation.

ARTCC—Air Route Traffic Control Center, an air-traffic control facility usually simply referred to as Center.

artificial horizon—A cockpit instrument which displays the attitude of the aircraft relative to the horizon.

ATC—Air Traffic Control.

AUS—Austin, Texas.

autopilot—A cockpit instrument which, by means of servo motors, flies the aircraft without manual help from the pilot.

BCE—Bryce Canyon, Utah.

Bellanca Super Viking—A high-performance single-engine aircraft produced by Bellanca Aircraft Corporation.

BLD—Boulder, Nevada.

Bonanza—A high-performance single-engine aircraft produced by Beech Aircraft Corporation.

BUM—Butler, Missouri.

carburetor heat—A means of feeding heated air into the carburetor to melt accumulations of carburetor ice.

Cardinal—A single-engine fixed-gear aircraft produced by Cessna Aircraft Company. Later models included a retractable-gear version. Production of the Cardinal family of aircraft has been discontinued.

cardinal altitudes—The altitudes at which VFR aircraft are required to fly when more than 3,000 feet above ground level. Cardinal altitudes for eastbound aircraft (0° to 179°) are odd thousands plus 500 feet. Cardinal altitudes for VFR aircraft westbound (180° to 359°) are even thousands plus 500 feet.

CAVU—Ceiling and visibility unlimited.

CBI—Columbia, Missouri.

CDC—Cedar City, Utah.

CDT—Central Daylight Time.

center—See ARTCC.

Centurion—A high-performance single-engine aircraft produced by Cessna Aircraft Company.

Century I—A simple autopilot produced by Edo-Aire/Mitchell.

Cessna—Cessna Aircraft Company, the largest producer of general-aviation aircraft.

CEZ—Cortez, Colorado.

Cherokee—A family of single-engine aircraft produced by Piper Aircraft Corporation.

Cherokee Arrow—See Arrow.

CLC—Course-line computer, a cockpit instrument used in area navigation.

CLL—College Station, Texas.

CNU—Chanute, Kansas.

com—Communications (equipment).

Comanche—A high-performance single-engine aircraft produced by Piper Aircraft Corporation. Production of the Comanche was discontinued some years ago.

com radio—communication radio, permitting two-way radio contact with ground facilities and other aircraft.

cones—Conical nerve-ends located in the center of the rear wall of the eye. The cones recognize color but are insensitive in conditions of average night-darkness.

control tower—Generally simply referred to as "tower," it houses the air-traffic control facilities which control traffic on and around a controlled airport.

COS—Colorado Springs, Colorado.

coupler—A means by which an autopilot can be coupled to a VOR or other ground-based navigation aid.

cruise-climb—Climbing at a higher-than-normal forward speed, producing an altitude gain of less fpm than would climbing at the best rate or best angle of climb.

deadstick landing—A landing with an inoperative engine (or, in twins, a landing with both engines inoperative).

DEN—Denver, Colorado.

DF steer—A means by which a ground-based ATC facility or flight-service station can determine the position of an aircraft in flight, and then guide it to an airport or back onto its course.

DG—Directional gyro (compass).

directional gyro—A compass which, once manually set, displays the direction of flight of the aircraft by means of a gyroscope. Directional gyros must be reset from time to time to continuously conform with the magnetic compass.

DME—Distance measuring equipment, a cockpit instrument which displays either the distance to or from a VORTAC, or the ground speed at which the aircraft is traveling. All DMEs display either nautical miles or knots. Some are also capable of displaying the time to the station (in minutes and tenth of minutes) at the current ground speed.

Edo-Aire/Mitchell—A manufacturer of a variety of autopilots and flight directors.
EMP—Emporia, Kansas.
EXT—East Texas VOR, Pennsylvania.

Falcon 20—A corporate jet produced by Avions Marcel Dassault-Breguet in France and marketed by Falcon Jet Aviation in the United States.
FBO—Fixed-base operator; an operation located on an airport and supplying tiedown, fuel, maintenance and other related services.
FMN—Farmington, New Mexico.
fpm—feet per minute (during climb or descent).
FSD—Sioux Falls, South Dakota.
FSS—Flight-service station.
FTZ—Foristell VOR, Missouri.

GCN—Grand Canyon, Arizona.
gph—Gallons per hour.
GUC—Gunnison, Colorado.
Gulfstream II—A corporate jet originally developed and produced by Grumman-American Corporation, now produced and marketed by Gulfstream-American Corporation.

HAR—Harrisburg, Pennsylvania.
HLV—Hallsville, Missouri.
HUB—Houston, Texas, Hobby Airport.
Hz—Hertz, the measure of radio frequencies.

IAH—Houston, Texas, International Airport.
IDU—Industry VOR, Texas.

134

IFR—Instrument flight rules, the air-traffic rules under which flight may be conducted in IFR conditions.

IFR conditions—Weather conditions which are below the ceiling and/or visibility minimums in which flight is permissible under visual-flight rules.

inertial navigation—A means of world-wide area navigation by means of a gyroscopic instrument which senses variations in the lateral movement of the aircraft and is capable of displaying the position of the aircraft at any time during the flight at any point of the globe.

INS—Inertial navigation system.

INW—Winslow, Arizona.

IOC—Kiowa VOR, Colorado.

ITC—Wichita, Kansas.

JEF—Jefferson City, Missouri.

Jeppesens—Aviation charts produced and marketed by Jeppesen-Sanderson.

JetStar—A four-engine corporate jet aircraft produced by Lockheed.

kHz—kilo Hertz, a measure of radio-wave frequencies.

knot—Nautical miles per hour.

LAS—Las Vegas, Nevada.

LBF—North Platte, Nebraska.

Learjet—A twin-engine corporate jet aircraft produced by Gates Learjet Corporation.

LOM—Locator outer marker, a ground-based navigation aid associated with instrument-approach systems.

MEA—Minimum en-route altitude; the minimum altitude at which the IFR flight may be conducted along an airway.

MEL—Multi-engine land; a pilot rating.

MHz—Mega Hertz; a measure of radio-wave frequencies.

Mitsubishi—A twin-turboprop aircraft produced partially by Mitsubishi Heavy Industries in Japan and partially by Mitsubishi Aviation in the United States; also know as MU-2.

mixture—The mixture of air and fuel which is needed to produce combustion in the engine. It must be adjusted by the pilot when changing flight altitudes.

MKT—Mankato, Minnesota.

MMM—Mormon Mesa, Nevada.

MOCA—Minimum obstacle-clearance altitude.

Mooney—A high-performance single-engine aircraft produced by Mooney Aircraft Corporation.

MRA—Minimum reception altitude; the minimum altitude at which reception of the signal from the applicable VOR can be assured.

msl—Mean sea level; the altitude above sea level.

MSP—Minneapolis, Minnesota.

nav—Navigation.

nav aid—A ground-based station emitting radio signals used by aircraft in flight for navigation.

nav-receiver—An aircraft radio designed to receive nav-aid signals.

NDB—Non-directional beacon, a low-frequency navigation aid.

nm—Nautical mile.

OBI—Omni-bearing indicator; a cockpit instrument displaying the position of the aircraft relative to a VOR.

OBS—Omni-bearing selector.

omni—Short for omni-directional very-high-frequency navigational radio range; a VOR.

ONL—O'Neill, Nebraska.

OSW—Oswego, Kansas.

OTG—Worthington, Minnesota.

PC—Positive control; a term used by Mooney Aircraft Corporation to denote the wing-leveler which is standard equipment on its aircraft.

PGA—Page, Arizona.

PGS—Peach Springs, Arizona.

PHX—Phoenix, Arizona.

pilotage—Navigating by ground features rather than radio.

Piper—Piper Aircraft Corporation, manufacturers of a large variety of general-aviation aircraft.

PIREPs—Pilot reports.

PUB—Pueblo, Colorado.

RNAV—Area navigation.

rods—Sensitive elements on the rear wall of the eye, surrounding the cones. Rods are color blind but have the ability to adjust to very low light levels and are therefore our means of night vision.

RON—Rest over night.

rpm—Revolutions per minutes.

RWF—Redwood Falls, Minnesota.

Sectional—An aviation chart published by the government. Scale: 1:500,000.

SEL—Single engine land; a pilot rating.

sequence reports—The hourly weather reports broadcast by flight-service stations at 15 minutes past the hour.

SGF—Springfield, Missouri.

sm—Statute mile.

stall—The condition resulting when an aircraft slows to the point at which it can no longer fly. It produces a sudden drop of the nose followed by an increase in airspeed. Inadvertent stalls can turn into a spin which, when happening close to the ground, is usually fatal.

STL—St. Louis, Missouri.

surveillance radar approach—A non-precision instrument approach in which the pilot is guided by instructions from a controller on the ground who watches his aircraft on radar. Also know as a GCA, ground-controlled approach.

TAS—True air speed.

TBC—Tuba City, Arizona.

TCA—Terminal control area; a portion of airspace around a major terminal in which all traffic is under positive ATC control.

TEB—Teterboro, New Jersey.

tetrahedron—A wedge-shaped or T-shaped rotating indicator located on airports to show pilots the direction of the wind.

TNV—Navasota, Texas.

TPL—Temple, Texas.

transponder—A cockpit instrument which replies to interrogation by ground-based radar and, in turn, causes the blip on the radar screen to stand out more clearly.

turn-and-bank indicator—A basic cockpit instrument showing the degree of bank and turn of the aircraft.

TXC—Thurman, Colorado.

uncontrolled airport—An airport without an operating control tower, or an airport with a control tower during the hours when the control tower is not being manned.

UNICOM—A ground-based two-way radio operated by FBOs or airport managers.

upper winds—Winds aloft.

VASI—Visual approach-slope indicator; a system of white and red lights installed on the airport to give the pilot positive indication of his position relative to the glide angle during final approach.

vector—Direction of flight based on instruction by a ground-based controller while handling an aircraft in radar contact, such as when an aircraft is being vectored to the outer marker.

VFR—Visual flight rules; the rules under which aircraft may operate without contact with ATC when the weather is above VFR minimums.

VFR conditions—Weather conditions with adequate ceilings and visibilities to permit aircraft to operate on the see-and-be-seen principle.

VFR flight plan—A flight plan filed for a VFR flight. It's purpose is to automatically activate search-and-rescue efforts if the aircraft fails to arrive at its destination.

Victor Airways—The system of airways based on the VOR network.

VIH—Vichy, Missouri.

VLF/Omega—A world-wide area-navigation system based on very-low-frequency radio waves.

VOR—Very high frequency omni-directional radio range; a network or ground-based navigation aids sending out signals which permit the pilot to determine his position relative to the station.

VORTAC—A combination VOR and TACAN, the latter being an added feature which is used by the on-board DME to determine distance from station and/or ground speed.

VSI—Vertical speed indicator; an instrument showing the rate of climb or descent in feet per minute.

WAC—World aeronautical chart; a series of aviation charts published by the government. Scale: 1:1,000,000.

wake turbulence—Air movement in the form of two counter-rotating horizontal tornadoes, created by the wing tips of heavy jet aircraft when oprating at low speeds. Technically all aircraft produce a degree of wake turbulence, but with other than heavy jets it is not a cause for concern.

waypoint—A term used in area navigation, denoting the location to which a VOR has been electronically moved.

winds aloft—Upper winds; the winds above 3,000 feet agl. Winds-aloft forecasts are available for altitudes in increments of 3,000 feet msl.

yoke—The "steering wheel" in an aircraft.

zero-zero conditions—Conditions of fog or other phenomena resulting in zero ceiling and zero visibility.

ZZV—Zanesville, Ohio.

Index